YOUR BRAIN IS LYING TO YOU

The Science of Rewiring Your Mind to Stop Overthinking, Conquer Fear, and End Self-Sabotage

EVAN SHAW

© Copyright 2025 – Evan Shaw
All rights reserved.

The content contained within this book may not be reproduced, duplicated, or transmitted without direct written permission from the author or the publisher.

Under no circumstances will any blame or legal responsibility be held against the publisher, or author, for any damages, reparation, or monetary loss due to the information contained within this book, either directly or indirectly.

Legal Notice:

This book is copyright protected. It is only for personal use. We cannot amend, distribute, sell, use, quote, or paraphrase any part, or the content within this book, without the consent of the author or publisher.

Disclaimer Notice:

Please note the information contained within this document is for educational and entertainment purposes only. All effort has been executed to present accurate, up-to-date, reliable, and complete information. No warranties of any kind are declared or implied. Readers acknowledge that the author is not engaged in the rendering of legal, financial, medical, or professional advice. The content within this book has been derived from various sources. Please consult a licensed professional before attempting any techniques outlined in this book.

By reading this document, the reader agrees that under no circumstances is the author responsible for any losses, direct or indirect, that are incurred as a result of the use of the information contained within this document, including, but not limited to, errors, omissions, or inaccuracies.

CONTENTS

INTRODUCTION 1

PART 1: The Problem 7

    Chapter 1: Your Brain is a Bad Roommate 9

    Chapter 2: Why You Can't Trust Your Instincts 26

    Chapter 3: The Comparison Trap 41

    Chapter 4: The Catastrophe Machine 59

PART 2: The Science of Change 79

    Chapter 5: Thoughts Are Just Chemicals 81

    Chapter 6: The Placebo Effect of Belief 102

    Chapter 7: How Your Memories Lie 117

    Chapter 8: The Myth of 'Positive Thinking' 135

PART 3: Breaking Free 155

    Chapter 9: The 90-Second Rule 157

    Chapter 10: Rewriting Your Mental Code 172

    Chapter 11: Why You're Addicted to Your Stories 189

    Chapter 12: The Truth About Control 209

CONCLUSION 226

REFERENCE 229

INTRODUCTION

You are lying to yourself.

Right now. Even as you read this, your brain is editing reality. Filling gaps. Hiding mistakes. Telling you the world makes sense when it doesn't. You think you're aware. You think you're in control. You're not.

Our minds are built to create coherent stories out of incomplete evidence, to see patterns that aren't there, to trust what we expect rather than what is real. We do it every day, sometimes in small ways, sometimes in ways that shape entire lifetimes.

I assure you, it's not just a theory or a quirk of perception; it has happened on a massive scale, to some of the smartest people alive.

In 1912, England celebrated what seemed to be the discovery of a "missing link," a fossilized skull that supposedly bridged apes and humans. It was perfect: exactly what scientists expected to find. The skull had a large braincase, as if intelligence had evolved first, and a primitive jaw, as if the body lagged behind. Museums displayed it proudly. Textbooks taught it. Lecturers spoke of it with certainty. Brilliant minds nodded along. For decades, it shaped how generations imagined human evolution.

Alas, it was a complete forgery. The skull was a human cranium, several hundred years old, and the jaw belonged to an orangutan. The teeth had been filed down to look human, and chemicals were used to age the bones. Someone went to painstaking lengths to fool the world.

Why? The motives are still debated. Some suspect Charles Dawson, the amateur archaeologist who "discovered" it, wanted fame and recognition. Others think it was a deliberate prank, a test of scientific gullibility. Whatever the reason, the result was the same: the lie persisted for forty years.

Here's the remarkable part: it wasn't just laypeople who were deceived. Some of the greatest scientists of the time examined the bones, debated their significance, and even defended them. They wanted to see a link that confirmed their theories. They looked at the evidence and accepted what they expected to see. Their brains filled in gaps, rationalized inconsistencies, and normalized what should have been impossible.

Every expert believed it. Every observer trusted their perception. Every brain—even yours, had you been there—would have been lying to itself. The Piltdown Man is a perfect example of how our minds can accept illusions as reality, how expectation, desire, and trust can override evidence, and how a single deception can shape what we assume to be truth for decades.

What's staggering about Piltdown isn't just the deceit itself, but how it mirrors what happens inside your own mind every day. Your brain doesn't wait for a hoax to trick you; it constructs its own, minute by minute, thought by thought. It fills in gaps when information is missing, edits memories so they make sense, and interprets events to confirm what you already believe.

Like those scientists who wanted a missing link, your brain wants stories that make the world predictable and comfortable, even if they're not true. It exaggerates threats, underplays strengths, rewrites encounters, and convinces you that your assumptions are facts, and you rarely notice.

Because these internal deceptions feel seamless, natural, normal. They shape your emotions, your decisions, and the way you see others without permission. Over time, repeated enough, the stories your brain tells become reality, a reality that feels inescapable, unquestionable, and true. This is why even brilliant, rational people can be fooled, why patterns that aren't there look obvious, and why the quiet, unnoticed lies of the mind are so powerful.

Just as the scientists saw what they expected, your brain shapes the world you experience to fit the stories you already tell yourself. Those stories can be trusted… or they can mislead you.

Your thoughts can either build you or bury you. The dangerous part is, most of us don't even realize which one is happening. We go through life reacting to things on the outside, deadlines, responsibilities, routines, rarely stopping to ask what's shaping everything from the inside. We obsess over strategy, over systems, over doing more. We major in the minors, pouring energy into little things while the big ones go unchallenged. We tweak our schedules, download new apps, change our morning routines, hoping one of those things will finally fix how we feel.

What we don't do is pause long enough to ask what we actually believe about ourselves. The thoughts are driving us. The quiet ones we've never challenged. The ones we've heard so often, they don't even sound like thoughts anymore. They just feel like reality.

Researchers at Queen's University ran a study using brain scans to track how often our minds jump from one thought to the next. Their 2020 findings suggest that the average person has around 6,000 distinct thoughts each day (Tseng et al., 2020). That's a lot of chances for your brain to feed you a story about who you are, what you can't do, why people pull away, and how nothing ever works out.

And here's the kicker: the brain doesn't treat all those thoughts equally. Psychologists have found that we tend to hold onto the negative ones more. The thoughts that make us feel rejected, unsafe, and not enough are the ones that stick (Baumeister et al., 2001). The brain sees them as useful, protective. It keeps them close just in case.

So most of what we think each day isn't new. It's recycled. Old fears. Old judgments. Old insecurities running on autopilot. So if you feel stuck, heavy, anxious, not good enough, there's a very real chance it's not your life that's broken. It's just the thoughts that have been running unchecked in the background.

Thoughts aren't passive. They shape everything including how you show up, how you speak, how you rest, how you relate, how you dream, how you love, how you pull away. You can't box them up neatly. They spill into places you don't expect. The ones you never question quietly become the rules you live by. The ones you keep repeating slowly become the filter you see through. Over time, without even realizing, they start to feel like who you are. Not because they're true. Just because your brain has fed them so many times, it thinks they must be safe.

This happens so often we stop noticing it. We start calling those thoughts personality traits. We say we're being careful, or humble, or just realistic. In reality, a lot of the time we're just following fear. A fear that's been repeating the same old story for years. One we've never had the language, or the space, to interrupt.

That's what this book is here for. I'm not trying to force you to think positive, or pretend hard things aren't happening. I need you to notice the version of reality your thoughts have been writing for you when you weren't paying attention. Doubt wasn't in your DNA. That came later. You weren't born scared to try, or rest, or speak, or ask, or take up space. That stuff got layered on, through repetition, through survival, through small moments that slowly made you smaller.

That story can be unlearned. The thoughts can be challenged. The loops can be broken.

I didn't write this as someone who figured it all out. I know what it's like to get everything right on the outside while everything inside feels like it's falling apart. I know what it's like to burn out and trace it back to one belief that's been in the background for years, a belief that never got questioned because it sounded so familiar, it almost became fact.

Your brain is smart. It's trying to protect you. The problem is, safe and stuck can feel the same when you don't slow down enough to notice. If you never stop to ask what's really driving you, your mind will build a life that doesn't actually fit you.

Your brain has been lying to you all along.

You don't have to live like that.

It's time to flip the script.

PART 1

The Problem

This part of the book isn't about working more. It's about seeing what's been working against you.

We're going behind the curtain to the hidden programs running the show. The thoughts you didn't choose. The fears that feel like facts. The mental noise you've mistaken for truth.

Because before you can change anything, you have to see the real enemy.

And it's not out there.

It's in here.

PART I

The Problem

1
Your Brain is a Bad Roommate

That's your best friend and your worst enemy - your own brain.
—**Fred Durst**

I used to have this roommate named Clark. Loud guy. Always yelling into his phone, playing music on speaker, banging around in the kitchen like he was hosting a cooking show. Morning, night, didn't matter. The whole apartment was always noisy.

The noise was bad, but honestly, the mess was worse. Clark would leave dirty dishes on the couch, half-eaten fast food on the counter, open cans of Red Bull sweating on the windowsill like decor. And once? A slice of bread on the bathroom sink. Just weird.

Living with him felt like waking up in a disaster I didn't cause. I'd come out of my room and instantly feel on edge, like my body braced itself before my brain caught up. The clutter got into everything, my energy, my mood, my focus. I was exhausted by 10 a.m. and hadn't even done anything yet.

Clark moved out eventually. The place got quiet again. Cleaner.

When I started learning how the brain actually works, and how much background activity runs even when you think you're resting, I couldn't help but think of Clark. The mind has its own version of Clark. A system that doesn't know how to be quiet, that leaves mental dishes all over the place, that keeps pulling you into old conversations and imagined disasters even when nothing's happening.

This chapter is about that roommate; the noise your brain makes when nothing's even happening. The mental clutter that shows up when you're trying to rest. The patterns you think are part of your personality, but might just be old wiring.

Let me show you just how bad of a roommate your brain can be.

The Default Mode Network

Most people assume their brain goes quiet when they're not doing anything. Like if you're lying on the couch or staring at the ceiling, you must be resting. That's not really how it works.

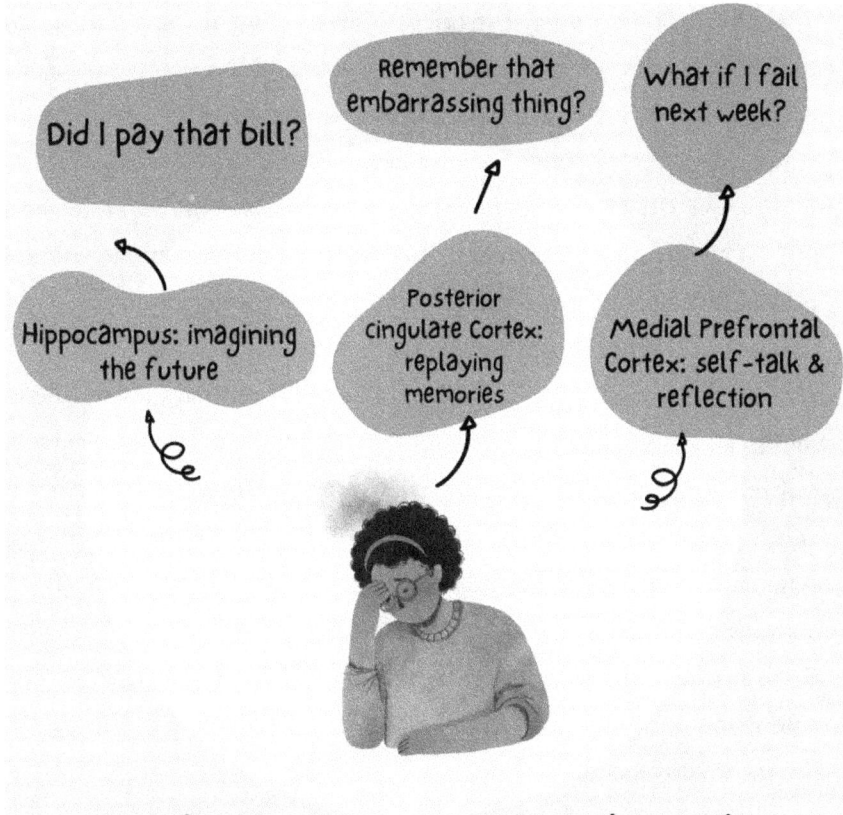

Default Mode Network (DMN)

Your brain has something called the *Default Mode Network*. People call it the DMN for short. It's a set of brain regions that light up when you're not focused on a specific task. So even if you're not moving, not talking, not "doing" anything, your brain is still running.

The DMN is what turns on when you're just thinking. Not thinking on purpose, like solving a math problem. More like mental background noise. Random thoughts. Daydreams. Replaying that weird thing you said in a meeting last week. Wondering if your friend is mad at you. Imagining how next week might go wrong. Remembering that one time in high school when you tripped in front of everyone. That kind of stuff.

In 2001, a neurologist named Marcus Raichle and his team published the first major study on the Default Mode Network. They discovered that even when a person isn't doing anything, no tasks, no problem-solving, no outside stimulation, parts of the brain are still highly active (Raichle et al., *Proceedings of the National Academy of Sciences*, 2001). This surprised researchers. Before then, they assumed the brain "powered down" when it wasn't busy.

Turns out, it doesn't. It just shifts into *internal* activity.

Since then, studies have shown that the DMN plays a key role in what's called self-referential thought, including how you see yourself, your relationships, and your future (Andrews-Hanna et al., *Frontiers in Human Neuroscience*, 2014). It's also linked to mind-wandering, imagination, daydreaming, and autobiographical memory, basically, all the ways you build and maintain a sense of identity.

It's not just one part of the brain. It's a network, meaning several regions in your brain are working together when you're in this mode. The most active areas include:

- The medial prefrontal cortex: involved in self-talk and personal reflection.
- The posterior cingulate cortex: linked to memory, internal storytelling, and pulling up past experiences.
- The hippocampus: handles memory and imagining future scenarios.
- A few other regions, such as the angular gyrus and lateral temporal cortex, also help tie meaning to your thoughts and language.

This network runs when you're "off task," which is most of the time. It's why you can sit down to rest and still feel mentally drained. Your body is still, but your brain is running laps.

Let me give you an example.

You ever closed your eyes to take a break, and your mind instantly jumps to that thing your cousin said last week? Or that bill you haven't paid yet? Or how awkward you felt at that birthday dinner? That's not random. That's the DMN.

If the Default Mode Network is so noisy, why do we even have it?

Simple answer: it helped us survive.

The DMN evolved as part of our brain's internal monitoring system. It keeps track of you, your memories, your fears, your regrets, your hopes. It helps you imagine the future, mentally rehearse conversations, think about how others see you, and reflect on past events. It's the part of the brain that lets you simulate life before you act in real time.

Basically, it tries to protect you from emotional and social harm by constantly predicting what could go wrong. In the right amount, that's useful. You need some level of reflection and anticipation. It helps you grow. Helps you learn. Helps you avoid making the same mistake twice.

The problem comes when the DMN shifts from useful monitoring to constant noise. When it becomes the default setting instead of something you can turn on and off. Most of us live in it *all the time*.

When the Default Mode Network stays switched on too much, it creates something called ruminative thinking, a kind of mental "chewing" where you keep turning over the same thoughts without actually getting anywhere (Nolen-Hoeksema et al., 2008). It feels like problem-solving, but it's not. You're just going in circles.

Over time, this constant mental activity becomes draining. Even if your day looked "easy" from the outside, the DMN has been burning fuel in the background, reviewing, predicting, judging, and editing.

That's why you can feel exhausted without having done anything visibly hard.

Here's the kicker: when the DMN is overactive, it actually interferes with your ability to be present. Studies show that increased DMN activity is linked to lower engagement in goal-directed tasks (Anticevic et al., 2012). It pulls attention inward, away from what's in front of you. So you might be trying to work, talk, or rest, but your brain keeps hijacking your focus to run the same old loops.

For people with anxiety or depression, this effect is even stronger. Functional MRI studies have found that hyperconnectivity in the DMN, especially in areas like the medial prefrontal cortex and posterior cingulate cortex, is associated with persistent negative self-focus and depressive rumination (Hamilton et al., 2011). In other words, the louder the DMN, the harder it is to break free from self-critical thoughts.

The brain has two major modes it flips between: one for *doing* and one for *wandering*. The doing mode is called the Central Executive Network; it's what you use when you're focused, solving a problem, getting stuff done. The wandering mode is the Default Mode Network, and it takes over when you're not actively concentrating on something outside of you.

These two systems can't run at the same time. It's like a seesaw. When one goes up, the other goes down.

This is why it's hard to focus. Your brain is in the wrong gear. You're trying to do something productive, but the DMN is still talking. About that awkward text. About how your boss probably hates you. About how you're not doing enough. It's like trying to write an email while someone's shouting in your ear.

Your mind can't engage with the task in front of you because it's already busy, just not in a way that helps you. If you've ever felt completely drained after a day where you "didn't do much," this is probably why. The DMN was running nonstop.

You might've been lying on the couch, but inside your head, you were arguing with someone, rehearsing a tough conversation, overanalyzing a weird comment, replaying the same moment from last week. That kind of thinking *feels* like rest, because you're not moving, but it's not. Your mind's still in overdrive.

This is what people mean when they say "I'm tired but I didn't do anything." Your brain's been burning mental fuel in the background all day.

You don't have to shut it down completely. You probably can't. The DMN isn't bad, it's just loud. It's there to help you reflect, remember, imagine. The goal isn't silence. It's *awareness*.

You want to notice when Clark is up to his usual tricks again?

That means catching yourself, naming what's happening. "Okay, my mind's replaying that thing again." Noticing without judgment is enough to take some of its power away.

You can also shift gears by changing what part of the brain you're using. The point isn't to suppress your thoughts. It's to stop letting that messy roommate run the whole place. You can start by just paying attention. Not to the thoughts themselves, but to the fact that they're happening at all.

That's usually the first real moment of quiet.

Negativity Bias: Evolution's Cruel Joke

Let's say five people give you feedback in one day. Four of them tell you that you did great. They say they liked your idea. They appreciated how you handled something. One of them, just one, says something slightly off. Maybe they say you talked too much in the meeting. Or your suggestion wasn't clear. Or your email felt "a bit much."

Guess which one your brain replays on the way home?

Not the compliments. Not the smiles or the thank-yous or the nods of agreement. Your brain grabs the one tiny drop of criticism and runs it on a loop like it's headline news. You'll hear that sentence in your head five, ten, maybe thirty times before you get home. You'll start editing your memory of the meeting. You'll wonder if everyone else secretly agreed. You might even start rewriting how you see yourself, all from one mild comment.

That's the negativity bias.

It is the brain's tendency to give more weight to negative experiences, thoughts, and information than positive ones (Baumeister et al., 2001). In practical terms, it means bad news is more pronounced. One harsh comment can cancel out ten kind ones. One mistake can feel bigger than dozens of wins.

This bias didn't come out of nowhere. It actually made a lot of sense, back when survival meant scanning the world for threats every second.

Let's say you are a human 100,000 years ago. You're out on the savannah, walking through tall grass. You hear a rustle. You have two options: ignore it, or assume it's dangerous. If it turns out to be just the wind and you got scared for no reason, you waste a few seconds. No big deal, but if it's a snake or a predator and you *don't* react? That could be the end of you.

So the brain evolved to treat anything negative, anything that might signal danger, like it's a five-alarm fire. Because back then, it probably was. Nice things were optional. Survival wasn't.

If you missed some juicy berries on a tree, that wasn't life-threatening. You'd find another tree, but if you missed the pattern of paw prints near the riverbank, or ignored the change in tone in someone's voice, or forgot the way a snake's scales looked in the sun, you didn't make it to the next day.

The humans who survived were the ones who paid *very* close attention to anything that felt off. So over thousands of years, the brain got better and better at noticing what could go wrong. That wiring got baked in.

Fast forward to now, and we still have the same system. Only now, the "threats" aren't lions or poisonous plants. They're texts that don't get replied to. Job applications that go ignored. That weird look someone gave you at the end of a meeting. That one word in someone's feedback that sounded off. Your brain doesn't know the difference. To it, emotional danger feels just as real as physical danger.

So it sounds the same alarm.

That explains why your mind zooms in on the one awkward comment instead of the ten good ones. It explains why you lie in bed replaying that one weird moment at the party. Why can you feel perfectly fine for most of the day, then suddenly lose it over a sentence someone said three years ago.

The problem is, we're not living in the wild anymore. We're not dodging tigers, but our brains never got the memo. So even though you're probably not fending off wild animals or sleeping with one eye open anymore, your nervous system still acts like it is. It keeps a mental log of everything that could hurt you, emotionally, socially, and physically, and holds it close.

The default mode network (DMN), which we talked about earlier, also comes into play here. Since the DMN is in charge of self-referential thinking, basically, thinking about yourself, it ends up being where a lot of these negative memories and fears get looped. If the DMN is already wired to scan your internal world, the negativity bias makes sure it scans for what's wrong.

Here's where it gets messier. Because your brain holds onto negative experiences more tightly, those memories become easier to access. That's called emotional salience; the more emotionally charged something is, the easier it is for your brain to pull it up again. So when you're in a low mood or anxious state, your brain serves up more of those negative memories and thoughts, reinforcing the cycle.

Over time, this becomes a loop. You feel bad → you think negative thoughts → those thoughts reinforce how bad you feel → your brain pulls up more bad stuff → you feel worse. It's just how the system was built.

Mental Clutter Vs Mental Clarity

Phone chargers wrapped around headphone wires, cords from devices you haven't used in years, all knotted together so tightly you don't even know where one starts and the other ends. You reach in to grab one thing, just one, and five other things come up with it. You end up spending ten minutes trying to free up the wire that you actually need, and when you eventually figure it out, you're irritated, tired, and late.

That's what it's like inside a cluttered mind.

Mental clutter is beyond "too many thoughts." It's when your thoughts are tangled and overlapping. When your brain's trying to track too many things at once: the conversation from yesterday, the email you forgot to send, the thing you're anxious about but can't name. You can't get to the thought you actually need because five others are stuck to it.

The worst part is that it never feels like you're doing anything. It feels like you're constantly *almost* doing something, opening tabs, developing half-finished ideas, looping back to things you thought you were done thinking about.

Mental clutter is the invisible kind of tiredness. You sit down after a typical day, exhausted, but you can't pinpoint what exactly wore you out so much. That's because your brain has been busy *all day*, just not in a useful way. You've been having full-blown conversations in your head, playing defense in imaginary arguments, jumping from thought to thought without actually landing anywhere.

It's that constant, low-grade noise that's running in the background, and trust me, it adds up. You forget things. You get irritable. Your sleep feels light and restless. You open a message and stare at it because even deciding what to respond with feels like a big chore.

You keep checking your phone not because you want to, but because your brain is searching for something, relief, distraction, certainty, dopamine, and it doesn't know how to rest without grabbing something. You get stuck for hours on end.

You open one app, scroll for a bit, close it, then open another one, like the first one didn't just disappoint you. You cycle through them without thinking. Instagram, Twitter, TikTok, maybe email. Even your Notes app, just to *check*. It's not a conscious decision. It's more like a twitch. A habit that feels soothing but doesn't actually soothe anything.

Sometimes your brain just wants to feel *different*. Lighter, less anxious, more certain about something, anything. So it goes looking, and the phone is always there, ready to offer just enough stimulation to quiet the discomfort for a second. Yet, it never really satisfies. It just keeps the engine running.

So even while you're scrolling, your mind is still spinning underneath. Thoughts piling on top of half-processed headlines, faces you don't know, things to buy, things to fix, things to worry about.

You picked up the phone to get away from the clutter in your head, but now your brain's even more overstimulated than before.

That makes you start to lose track of what you're actually feeling. Because when every emotion is layered on top of another, they start bleeding together. A little shame gets wrapped up in anxiety. A bit of grief clings to frustration. You don't know what you need. You just know something feels off.

Your brain is wired to hold on to this kind of noise. It hates open loops. It's called the Zeigarnik Effect; your brain will keep rehearsing unresolved or incomplete things, even when you're not trying to. That's useful when it helps you remember to call the bank. It's not so helpful when it traps you in a cycle of replaying the exact same worry for the 12th time.

Now contrast that with mental clarity.

Mental clarity doesn't mean peace and quiet all the time. It's not some Zen ideal. It just means the cords are laid out. The thoughts are still there, the stress, the to-do list, the conversation you're nervous about, but they're not piled on top of each other. You can see what you're working with.

You're not flipping between five playlists and a podcast at once. You can finish one thought before the next one interrupts. You can hear your actual instincts again, instead of all the noise trying to shout over them.

Mental clarity makes space. It gives your thoughts room to breathe. It lets you *choose* what to focus on, instead of having your focus dragged around by whatever thought is screaming the loudest. It lets you respond instead of react.

Clarity doesn't just show up. It's something you have to come back to. Like tidying up your room, or resetting your desk at the end of the day. The goal isn't to have a permanently silent mind. It's important to notice when the cords are starting to tangle again and take a moment to untangle them before they wrap around everything.

That might look like writing things down. Take a walk without your phone. Naming what you're actually feeling instead of letting the emotion stew. Sometimes the reset is small, like one deep breath before you open your inbox. Sometimes it's bigger, like stepping away from a screen and letting your nervous system slow down.

Your Brain as a Pattern-Matching Machine

I found this antique crocheting machine at a museum once, not the hand-held kind with tiny hooks, but this big, clunky machine made of metal and wood and sharp little gears. The part that fascinated me most was how it used these stiff punch cards, each of which had holes punched into it in a certain pattern. You'd slide a card into the machine, and once it was threaded with yarn, it would just follow that pattern over and over again, row by row. Same loop, same stitch, same shape. The machine didn't know what it was making. It didn't know if it was beautiful or not. It just ran the card.

Our brains aren't so different. Your brain is a pattern-matching machine. It takes whatever you experience, a look, a tone, a smell, a sentence, a pause, and tries to match it to something it's seen before. The idea is to make sense of the world quickly. The brain doesn't necessarily wait around to analyse; it reacts. Fast.

This is how you know how to drink from a cup without thinking. Or why you instinctively flinch when you hear shouting, even if no one's shouting *at* you. It's why you tense up when someone reminds you of your dad, or why a harmless balloon popping can make your chest tighten if your brain once filed that sound under "danger."

That automatic matching is what helps us survive. If a newborn baby had to "figure out" how to eat, it wouldn't last very long. Instead, it's born with a hardwired pattern match, mouth on nipple equals food. Even if the nipple isn't real, that's the reason a baby will also try to suck on a bottle teat, or even someone's finger. Close enough. The brain runs the card.

Not all pattern matches are bad. Many are adaptive. They're what allow us to move through the world without stopping to relearn everything from scratch, but not all of them are accurate. When the brain makes the wrong match, it leads to what therapists call a faulty pattern match.

Let's say you had a panic attack once while giving a presentation. Your brain may now associate *any* situation where you're being watched with fear. Job interviews, birthday toasts, and even introducing yourself in a group. It's automatic; the brain sees the social pressure and runs the card labeled "DANGER."

Same with people who fear dogs, or flying, or rejection. Or why some people get sexually aroused by things that don't make logical sense. Somewhere along the way, the brain accidentally paired that thing with a strong emotional response. That emotional glue made the link stick, and now it plays on a loop.

This kind of matching is often shaped during emotional or high-stress moments. That's because strong emotion locks attention, and attention is what creates those mental punch cards in the first place. That's also why hypnosis and trauma both tap into this mechanism. The brain becomes more suggestible under emotional intensity. It absorbs whatever happens in that state, files it, and uses it as a template going forward.

It doesn't have to be dramatic either. Sometimes, all it takes is repetition. You get rejected a few times, and you start a pattern of matching every close relationship with potential abandonment. You fail in a few public situations, and now "being seen" feels threatening.

Even a quiet sigh from someone else might trigger a memory your brain labeled as shame.

The brain doesn't just look for patterns; it *prefers* them. It would rather run an old, familiar script than sit with uncertainty. It would rather assume someone is mad at you than hold the possibility that you don't know how they feel. That's why you can feel stuck in loops that don't make sense.

Quiet ≠ Peace

We tend to mix them up. If a place is quiet, we assume it must be peaceful. If a person is sitting still, we think they must be at ease. Quietness and peace are not the same thing; they're sisters, not twins.

Quietness is external. It's the absence of noise, the hush of a library, the stillness of a street at 3 a.m., the moment after the kettle clicks off. It's when the outside world stops throwing sounds and movement at you.

Peace is internal. It's the calm in your chest, the looseness in your jaw, the softening of the mind when it stops rehearsing worst-case scenarios. Peace is what you feel when you're not bracing for something, when you're not trying to control the next moment.

You can have one without the other.

- **Quiet without peace**

You're lying in bed at night. The room is dark, the house is silent, but your mind is replaying a conversation from earlier, twisting it into a thousand "what if" scenarios. It's quiet out there, but inside? Chaos.

Or you're in a cabin in the woods, no Wi-Fi, no traffic, but you can't stop checking your phone for a signal, as if the Internet might return with the answer to whatever's gnawing at you.

- **Peace without quiet**

You're at a crowded family gathering, kids shrieking in the background, dishes clattering in the sink, and yet you're sitting on the porch, feeling completely at ease. The noise is just part of the scenery.

Or you're in a busy café, laptop open, music playing, voices overlapping, and somehow, your mind is still. The bustle doesn't touch you.

The reason we confuse the two is that quietness can be a doorway to peace. When the outer world softens, it's easier to hear yourself, to unclench. However, if the noise is in your head, no amount of silence outside will fix it.

It's like a snow globe. When you shake it, the flakes swirl around wildly, your thoughts, your worries, your long to-do list. Setting the snow globe down (quietly) stops the shaking, but the flakes (your mental chatter) don't settle right away. Peace comes when the flakes drift to the bottom and the water clears. That part takes time, and it happens inside.

The trouble is, when the outside world finally stops, you can no longer blame its chaos for your own. The hum you wanted to escape, the restlessness, the arguments, the unfinished thoughts, don't live out there. They live right here with you.

Chapter Summary

- The DMN evolved as part of our brain's internal monitoring system. It keeps track of you, your memories, your fears, your regrets, and your hopes. It's the part of the brain that lets you simulate life before you act in real time.
- The negativity bias is the brain's tendency to give more weight to negative experiences, thoughts, and information than

positive ones. In practical terms, it means bad news is more pronounced.

- Mental clarity doesn't mean peace and quiet all the time. It's not some Zen ideal. The thoughts are still there, the stress, the to-do list, the conversation you're nervous about, but they're not piled on top of each other. You can see what you're working with.

2

Why You Can't Trust Your Instincts

> "Where instinct fails, intellect must venture."
> —**Jim Butcher,** Storm Front

A couple of years ago, I got on a late-night flight and instantly decided the guy sitting next to me was trouble. I couldn't prove it. I just "felt it." He was fidgety, looking around a lot, and kept digging through his backpack. My brain went straight into detective mode. *Why's he acting weird? What's in the bag? Should I tell someone?*

For the first twenty minutes, I sat there on edge. I barely moved, barely made eye contact. I was convinced my instincts were picking up on something dangerous.

Then the flight attendant came by, and he asked if she had any ginger ale. He told her he gets motion sickness and always feels nervous before takeoff. It turns out that the "suspicious" bag rummaging was him looking for ginger candies. The constant glancing around? He was trying to distract himself from feeling nauseous.

I'd built this whole dramatic scenario in my head, and the truth was... the guy just didn't want to throw up on me.

That's the thing about instincts: they feel like they're giving you the truth, but a lot of the time, they're just your fears dressing up as facts.

In 2020, Stanford University researchers studied children with high anxiety. Using brain scans, they discovered that the amygdala (the brain's threat detector) was sending strong, urgent signals to the prefrontal cortex, the part responsible for logic and planning, but the signals going in the other direction were weak.

Translation: fear was yelling, and logic wasn't yelling back.

This is the same mechanism psychologist Daniel Goleman calls an *amygdala hijack*. When the amygdala senses a threat, it acts first and fast, triggering a rush of adrenaline, a spike in heart rate, tense muscles, and tunnel vision. The logical brain is slower. By the time it's ready to weigh the facts, the emotional brain has already decided how you should feel and what you should do.

Neuroscientist Antonio Damasio's *Somatic Thompsoner Hypothesis* explains why this is so profound: your brain links certain bodily sensations, like a racing heart or tight chest, to danger. The next time you feel them, it assumes you're in trouble, even if nothing is actually wrong.

Here's the dangerous part: every time you act on that fear, you're reinforcing the pathway. Your brain takes your reaction as proof that the fear was justified. That's how you end up in the Fear Loop, a cycle where fear reacts first, logic gets sidelined, and your responses become faster and more automatic each time.

It doesn't matter if the "threat" is a fidgety passenger, a tense meeting request, or a friend taking too long to reply to your message. The process in your brain is the same. Fear pulls the fire alarm, logic gets drowned out, and you start making decisions based on what you feel, not what's true.

The Fear Loop

In the late 1960s and early 1970s, psychologist Martin Seligman conducted a series of experiments that changed how we understand fear, trauma, and helplessness. His research involved dogs placed in situations where they were exposed to mild electric shocks they couldn't escape.

Some dogs were able to avoid the shocks by jumping over a small barrier to a safe side of the cage. Others were restrained, forced to endure the shocks with no way out. Later, when all dogs were put in a cage where escape was possible, those who had control before quickly learned to jump to safety but the dogs who had been trapped and helpless didn't even try. They had learned that no matter what they did, they couldn't escape, so they stopped trying.

This phenomenon became known as *learned helplessness*, a condition where the brain gets stuck in a cycle of fear and passivity because it believes escape or change isn't possible.

This is quite similar to what happens when you are caught in a loop of fear. When you face repeated uncontrollable stress, your brain can build an invisible cage, a loop of fear and helplessness that keeps you stuck long after the danger is gone.

This time, the cages aren't made of metal bars but of neural pathways shaped by fear, trauma, and experience. When your brain encounters danger or pain repeatedly, it adapts by creating shortcuts, patterns designed to help you react quickly.

At the core of this loop is the amygdala, found in your temporal lobes. The amygdala is essentially your brain's rapid-response danger detection system. It receives sensory data (sights, sounds, smells) directly from the thalamus and, in some cases, bypasses the slower, analytical pathways. This shortcut is why you can recoil from a shadow before realizing it's just a tree branch.

When the amygdala determines something might be dangerous, it triggers the hypothalamic–pituitary–adrenal (HPA) axis. The hypothalamus signals the pituitary gland, which in turn prompts the adrenal glands to release adrenaline and cortisol. Adrenaline boosts heart rate, blood pressure, and respiration, priming your muscles for action. Cortisol mobilizes glucose into the bloodstream, ensuring you have the energy to fight, flee, or freeze.

So far, this is adaptive, your survival depends on it. However, there are some cases where the loop can turn toxic:

- **The Prefrontal Cortex Weakens:** The prefrontal cortex is designed to regulate the amygdala. It interprets context, evaluates risks, and can inhibit fear responses when they're

unnecessary. Chronic stress, however, can impair prefrontal function, reducing its ability to apply the brakes.
- **The Hippocampus Loses Context:** The hippocampus provides the spatial and temporal context for memories. It tells you whether the rustle in the bushes is *now dangerous*, or just a memory from last summer. Prolonged cortisol exposure can physically damage hippocampal neurons, shrinking its volume and weakening its ability to provide that context.
- **Neuroplasticity Reinforces the Loop:** Each time your amygdala launches a fear response and it goes unchallenged, the synaptic connections in that circuit are strengthened. Over time, this creates a well-trodden neural pathway where fear becomes the default response, even in safe environments.

In plain terms, here's what that all means: imagine your brain has a smoke alarm (the amygdala) that's meant to go off only when there's a real fire. In a healthy system, the "building manager" (your prefrontal cortex) can check and say, "False alarm, it's just burnt toast," while the "security cameras" (your hippocampus) confirm it's not the same kitchen fire from last year.

Now, when you've been through repeated stress or trauma, the smoke alarm starts going off at every little puff of steam. The manager gets too exhausted to intervene, the cameras get blurry, and the alarm wiring gets so reinforced that it rings at the slightest hint of heat, even when you're perfectly safe. That's the fear loop: your brain reacting as if the danger never ended, even though the fire's long gone.

The hardest part is that once these fear cages form, the brain doesn't just dismantle them when the threat disappears. Instead, it leans on the old, familiar patterns because they feel "safe", or at least predictable.

Just like Seligman's dogs who didn't try to escape the cage after the barrier was removed, your brain clings to these fear loops. You avoid situations or people that trigger anxiety, or your mind might race with worst-case scenarios even when there's no real threat. It feels like there's an invisible ceiling or boundary holding you back, even though the walls aren't there anymore. The fear loop convinces you the cage is still locked tight.

So, how do you identify this loop? The fear loop is a cycle, it often feels like you're stuck in a fog of anxiety, but without seeing what's causing it. Here's how you spot it:

- **Physical signs:** Racing heart, shallow breathing, muscle tension, sweating, nausea, or an urge to escape.
- **Mental signs:** Racing thoughts, obsessive worries, imagining worst-case scenarios, replaying conversations or failures.
- **Behavioral signs:** Avoidance of certain people, places, or tasks; procrastination; feeling "paralyzed" or stuck.
- **Emotional signs:** Feeling overwhelmed, on edge, irritable, or numb.

If you notice these happening repeatedly, especially when there's no immediate danger, you might be in the fear loop. Another way is to track your triggers. What kinds of thoughts or situations kick off the loop? The more you notice patterns, the better you can spot the cycle

The fear loop can sneakily invade every part of your life, your work, relationships, health, and happiness. When fear controls your decisions, you:

- Miss opportunities because you're too scared to try.
- Avoid meaningful relationships out of mistrust or anxiety.

- Struggle with concentration and productivity.
- Experience chronic stress that wears down your body and mind.
- Get stuck in isolation or depression.

The loop becomes a prison. You're living under the shadow of your own fear, replaying the past or worrying about the future so much that you miss the present. It's not just a "mental problem." It can cause real, lasting damage if left unchecked.

The thing is… your fear loop isn't happening in isolation. It's not some mysterious quirk, it's plugged directly into the way your brain processes *all* decisions. The amygdala shortcut is basically your brain's "System 1". Lightning fast, instinctive, and convinced it's protecting you from disaster.

That same system that saves your life when a car runs a red light can also keep you trapped when there's no real danger at all. The only way to spot the difference is to know when to hand the wheel over to your slower, more deliberate thinking, what psychologists call "System 2."

In other words: to escape the fear loop, you need to learn how to switch gears between *fast* and *slow* thinking. Let me show you how it works.

Fast Vs Slow Thinking (System 1 Vs System 2)

It was supposed to be a simple errand. Thompson stood in the cereal aisle, scanning the shelves. He knew he wanted something healthy. He also knew he didn't want to spend more than $5. Yet, ten minutes later, he was still standing there, frozen, holding two boxes in his hands, running price, calorie–taste equations in his head like some overworked accountant. Meanwhile, a few aisles over, his wife effortlessly tossed shampoo, apples, and coffee into the cart without thinking twice.

Later that day, Thompson almost stepped into the street without looking, until a blaring horn yanked him back to the curb. That time, there was no hesitation. No analysis.

Two situations. Two completely different speeds of thinking. That's because your brain runs on *two systems*, one fast, automatic, and intuitive; the other slow, deliberate, and analytical.

In 2011, psychologist Daniel Kahneman, winner of the Nobel Prize in Economics, introduced the world to a simple but powerful idea in his bestselling book *Thinking, Fast and Slow*: your brain operates in two modes.

- System 1 is *fast, automatic, intuitive*. It's always on, scanning your environment, jumping to conclusions, and helping you get through life without getting bogged down in analysis. It's what stops you from touching a hot stove, makes you flinch when a ball flies toward your face, and lets you read this sentence without consciously sounding out each letter.

    System 1 runs on *patterns, shortcuts, and emotional signals*. It's your survival autopilot.
- System 2 is *slow, deliberate, logical*. It's what you engage in when you solve a math problem, write an essay, or decide between job offers. It's effortful. It burns more mental energy. And, here's the kicker, it's *lazy*. It doesn't want to turn on unless absolutely necessary.

Most of your life is run by System 1. System 2 is like the responsible but reluctant older sibling who only steps in when things get complicated.

The two systems are partners but the partnership is flawed. System 1 gets you through most moments quickly, but it can also be biased, overconfident, and wrong. System 2 is accurate and logical, but it's slow and easily fatigued.

Kahneman and Amos Tversky's decades of research revealed that many of our worst decisions happen when we let System 1 dominate situations that require System 2, and when we fail to notice our biases.

In a famous 2003 study, Princeton and University of Michigan psychologists gave participants a *Cognitive Reflection Test* (CRT), three deceptively simple math problems designed to trip up System 1.

Here's one of them (don't rush):

> A bat and a ball cost $1.10 in total.
> The bat costs $1.00 more than the ball.
> How much does the ball cost?

Most people immediately blurt out 10 cents. That's System 1 jumping in, it feels right, but it's wrong. If the ball cost 10 cents, the bat would cost $1.10, making the total $1.20. The correct answer is 5 cents.

To get there, you had to slow down, check the math, and engage System 2.

What's fascinating? Across multiple studies, over 50% of students at top universities got at least one of the three CRT questions wrong. Even intelligent, educated people are vulnerable to System 1's quick but flawed thinking.

Don't get me wrong, System 1 isn't the villain. It's the reason you can:

- Instantly recognize a friend's face in a crowd
- Catch a glass before it falls off the counter

- Slam the brakes when a child runs into the road

In emergencies, System 1's speed is a lifesaver. The problem is when it plays hero in situations where accuracy matters more than speed.

System 2, for all its virtues, can also fail you. Ever spent so long analyzing a decision that you missed the opportunity altogether? That's analysis paralysis, System 2 getting stuck in overthinking. Or maybe you've felt mentally exhausted after a day of problem-solving, that's decision fatigue.

Kahneman's research makes it clear: You can't turn off System 1, and you wouldn't want to but you can train yourself to notice when it's likely to be wrong and call in System 2 for backup.

Here are some signs that you're likely in fast thinking mode:

- You feel certain instantly
- You rely on gut feelings without checking facts
- You use stereotypes or assumptions
- You react emotionally before thinking

Even more signs that you need to switch to slow thinking:

- The stakes are high (career, finances, relationships)
- The problem is new or unfamiliar
- You have conflicting information
- Your gut reaction feels *too* easy

I'll give you a little exercise that will help you learn to switch between System 1&2. Over the next week:
1. Spot System 1 moments: Notice when you make snap judgments. It could be about a person you just met, a headline you read, or a quick financial choice.

2. Pause and Probe: Ask yourself:
   - *What assumptions am I making?*
   - *What information am I missing?*
3. Engage System 2: Spend just two extra minutes analyzing before deciding. You'll be amazed how often your second thought beats your first.

One more CRT puzzle for you. Here's another famous one (don't answer instantly):

> In a lake, there's a patch of lily pads.
> Every day, the patch doubles in size.
> If it takes 48 days for the patch to cover the entire lake, how long would it take for the patch to cover half the lake?

Most people say "24 days" (System 1). The correct answer? 47 days. On day 47, it's half the lake; the next day, it doubles to full.

Micro Dangers, Macro Responses

If we rewind 200,000 years, micro dangers wouldn't exist. Back then, most of what threatened us was macro by default: predators, hostile weather, rival tribes. You either saw the lion in the tall grass or you didn't make it to dinner.

Our nervous systems evolved to overshoot rather than undershoot responses. Think of it like a Formula 1 car that slams from zero to 200 mph in three seconds. In the wild, that was perfect. In an open-plan office or a Zoom meeting? Not so much.

Researchers at NYU have demonstrated how easily the system overgeneralizes. In one study, people learned to associate a particular shape with a mild electric shock. Later, they reacted with fear to shapes that only looked vaguely similar, even though those were harmless. Once the brain learns a danger pattern, it's quick to shout "close enough."

The problem is that constant false alarms add up. Psychologists who track daily hassles find they often have a bigger cumulative effect on stress than single major life events. The micro triggers are relentless. Each one siphons off a little patience, a little focus, a little immune resilience.

If your brain treats every late text, every unexpected sound, every ambiguous facial expression as a signal to brace for impact, you never fully come down. That's like keeping a car engine at high revs all day. Eventually, something burns out.

Your nervous system can't easily tell the difference between a small threat and a big one. It's like an airport scanner that beeps for both knives and belt buckles. In neuroscience, this lowering of the danger threshold is called sensitization. The more often your amygdala fires, the easier it becomes to set it off.

That's why a veteran can flinch at fireworks. Why is someone who has been ill tensed at the first cough? Why one bad breakup can make every new conversation feel risky.

Reversing this pattern takes deliberate work. One step is noticing it in real time. For a few days, you can jot down moments when your reaction feels larger than the trigger deserves. What set it off? How did it feel in your body? How quickly did you realize you were safe?

Another step is to intervene at the body level before your brain spins out. Breathing techniques work here because they tell your system "you are safe" before your thoughts have a chance to argue. Slow inhales, long exhales, and deliberate pauses between them send strong, calming signals.

Finally, you can retrain the system by exposing yourself to mild, safe discomforts on purpose. Speak up in a meeting. Send the message you've been avoiding. Take the slower lane in traffic. These moments teach your amygdala that tension doesn't always predict disaster. Over time, it learns to stand down.

The goal isn't to erase your macro response, that's a survival feature. It's to restore proportion. You still need to launch into full alert if a real threat shows up. However, when your body treats a text message like a tiger, you're living in a constant siege state that serves no one.

A healthy nervous system can tell the difference between a lion and a laptop notification. It can distinguish between a storm on the horizon and a passing cloud. When it does, life stops feeling like one long false alarm.

The Logic Deactivation Phenomenon

Sometimes, your thinking brain just packs up and leaves without warning, like a roommate who decides to take a weekend trip without telling you.

Think of it like a power outage. The building (you) is still standing. The walls are fine. However, the lights have flickered off, the appliances won't run, and somewhere in the electrical panel, a breaker has tripped. The circuits for logic have temporarily gone offline.

So why does it happen?

The case: "The Mysterious Disappearance of Rational Thought." The suspects?

First on the list: Emotional Hijack. This is when your amygdala, the emotional command center, decides it's got a more important message than whatever your prefrontal cortex (logic HQ) was working on. It floods your system with signals that scream "react now," and suddenly your rational circuits are drowned out.

Second suspect: Blood Flow Diversion. Your brain can't give VIP treatment to every region at once. Under stress, even low-level stress like being watched or having a ticking clock, more blood gets redirected toward survival-oriented systems. That means less oxygen and energy for higher reasoning.

Third suspect: Working Memory Overload. This is the "too many tabs open" problem. Your prefrontal cortex can only juggle so much. Add one more thing, a noise, a deadline, a stray worry, and the whole system crashes.

Put together, these suspects make a compelling case. The logic center isn't broken. It's just on a forced coffee break because the emotional team yelled too loud, the energy budget got slashed, and the desk was buried in paperwork.

The logic deactivation phenomenon has a nasty feedback loop. When you realize you're failing to think clearly, the sense of urgency spikes, which fuels more stress, which further suppresses logical capacity. You can get into complete cognitive gridlock.

Military and emergency responders train specifically to resist this. They use stress inoculation, deliberately practicing skills under high-pressure, high-noise, high-adrenaline conditions, to keep the prefrontal cortex engaged. In law enforcement training, officers may be asked to solve math problems while someone shouts at them, simulating the cognitive interference of real danger.

But for everyday life, you don't need boot camp to break the cycle. You need techniques that restore oxygen and blood flow to the brain's higher centers.

So how do you flip the breaker back on? Here are three counterintuitive approaches:

1. Do something slightly absurd.

Your brain loves novelty. If you suddenly start reciting your phone number backward or imagining what a zebra would look like in a business suit, you jolt your mind out of autopilot and give logic a hook to climb back in.

2. Change your physical state.

Stand up. Sit differently. Walk three steps away and come back. This sends new sensory data to your brain, forcing it to recalibrate.

3. Ask a fact question.

Something totally unrelated to the problem at hand. "What's the capital of Norway?" "What year did the moon landing happen?" This reroutes neural traffic toward knowledge recall, which often re-engages the prefrontal cortex.

The beauty of these is that they're quick, they're weird, and they work. They break the micro-shutdown before it becomes a macro-meltdown.

Chapter Summary

- When you face repeated uncontrollable stress, your brain can build an invisible cage, a loop of fear and helplessness that keeps you stuck long after the danger is gone.
- A healthy nervous system can tell the difference between a lion and a laptop notification. It can distinguish between a storm on the horizon and a passing cloud. When it does, life stops feeling like one long false alarm.
- When you're calm, it's easy to think things through. You can weigh options, consider details, and make decisions that actually make sense.

3

The Comparison Trap

> "Other people's lives seem better than yours because you're comparing their director's cuts with your behind-the-scenes."
> — Evan Rauch

Caroline Koziol was once a rising swimming talent in Glastonbury, Connecticut, a freshman who shattered her school's 100-yard butterfly record and seemed destined for collegiate competition. Then came the pandemic. The pools were closed, training stopped, and Caroline's life shifted from the water to her phone.

At first, social media was a welcome distraction. She browsed recipes, watched workout tips, and connected with friends. However, soon, Instagram and TikTok's algorithms began feeding her something else entirely, an endless stream of extreme diet advice, "fitspiration" content, and body-comparison posts. What began as harmless scrolling turned into a steady diet of toxic ideals.

By her senior year, Caroline's health had collapsed. She had lost about 30 pounds in twelve months. A typical day's food might be a protein bar, a few baby puffs, and a Diet Coke. She purged so often that she kept mascara and paper towels in her car to mask the evidence. Her once-strong body was so weak she nearly fainted during swim practice in September 2021.

The toll was physical and mental: her teeth and throat were damaged, her hormones were disrupted, her memory dulled. She described herself as "like a zombie." Even after entering treatment, first outpatient, then intensive care at a Monte Nido facility, the same harmful content kept appearing in her feed. As she put it, "The second I click on it, I know I'll see more tomorrow."

Now a junior at the University of Hartford, Caroline is one of the named plaintiffs in a sweeping legal action against Meta (Instagram) and ByteDance (TikTok). She and more than 1,800 others, including parents, school districts, and nearly 30 state attorneys general, allege that these platforms are "addictive and dangerous by design." They argue the companies' algorithms exploit brain chemistry to maximise engagement, at the expense of users' mental and physical health.

The lawsuit seeks damages and structural reforms: safer design features, transparent algorithms, and stronger protections for minors. While a judge has allowed key claims like negligence and product liability to proceed, the companies are expected to mount aggressive defences under Section 230, which shields platforms from liability for user-generated content.

For Caroline, the legal fight is personal. She chose to stay local for university, putting recovery ahead of her swimming ambitions. She has drastically limited her social media use, blocked triggering content, and replaced intense exercise with gentler, mindful movement. Her goal is twofold: to reclaim her own health and to hold accountable the industry she believes nearly destroyed it.

Her case is now a flashpoint in a growing debate about social media's impact on young people, a vivid example of how the promise of connection can be warped into an engine of comparison, compulsion, and harm.

Caroline's story is proof of how precisely these platforms know how to keep you hooked. Every swipe, every like, every "suggested post" was a calculated hit to her brain's reward system, pulling her deeper into the mess.

It's called dopamine hijacking. She was caught in a constant social mirror, measuring herself against faces and bodies that weren't even real in the first place. In the process, she slipped into digital overidentification, where the person in her reflection stopped feeling like her and started feeling like a project to be fixed. The goal? The "better me" illusion, that shimmering promise that if she just worked harder, ate less, and pushed more, she could finally become enough.

Maybe you know that feeling. The fear. The anxiety. The restlessness when you're offline. The way your skin can suddenly feel like the wrong size. The way confidence evaporates when you scroll through other people's perfect days. Someone once said we're only as perfect as our camera lenses. And those lenses? They lie. Every single time.

Dopamine Hijacking

You can get addicted to your phone the same way people get addicted to drugs. You wake up, and the first thing you do is check your notifications. Fifteen minutes later, you've scrolled through dozens of posts, liked a few photos, and watched a couple of videos you barely remember.

Before you know what is happening, you've spent a whole hour on your phone, yet, you can't seem to put it down. This is more than just a habit, it's a form of addiction caused by your brain's reward system being hijacked.

In the case of drugs, your brain gets blasted with chemicals that make you feel good, and then it starts craving that high. Phones don't inject chemicals, but every like, notification, or new post triggers the same reward system, tiny bursts of dopamine that tell your brain, "Do it again." Over time, your brain starts chasing those hits compulsively. You scroll without thinking, ignore everything else, and feel restless when you can't check your phone, like someone craving a fix.

Dopamine is central to the brain's reward system. It's released when we experience something pleasurable, reinforcing behaviors that lead to those pleasures. Social media platforms exploit this by providing an endless stream of new content, each piece potentially rewarding. This setup creates a "variable reward" system, similar to a slot machine, where the unpredictability of the next reward keeps you coming back.

Research has shown that this kind of stimulation can lead to changes in brain structure and function. For instance, a study by

Swinburne University found that just three minutes of social media use can decrease brain activity and focus in young adults. The research monitored participants' brain activity in the prefrontal cortex (the area responsible for cognitive control and decision-making) while engaging in different types of screen time: social media, mobile gaming, and television. Social media caused an initial influx of oxygen without subsequent brain function, suggesting wasted cognitive resources. Participants who showed this brain pattern also felt less focused. (Swinburne University, 2024)

The effects of constant digital stimulation go way beyond just being "distracted." It's not just that you lose an hour scrolling Instagram or YouTube, your brain starts to change, bit by bit, without you even noticing. When we're consistently flooded with notifications, posts, videos, and messages day after day, our brains start adapting negatively. Studies show that too much screen time can actually alter the way we process information, and those changes show up in almost every part of our daily lives.

Think about how easy it is to scroll endlessly. Every post, every video, every little notification is a mini-reward. Over time, your brain starts expecting that constant novelty. That means sitting down to read a book, focus on a project, or even just listen in a conversation can feel unbearable. Your mind drifts more easily, you fidget, and it's harder to stick with anything that doesn't give instant feedback.

Flitting from one post to the next, from video to video, can feel like learning or keeping up, but your brain isn't really storing much. This superficial engagement weakens memory retention. You might "know" a lot of things on the surface, but as soon as someone asks you to recall details, it's gone. Little facts, instructions, even things you wanted to remember, poof, gone. You end up forgetful, scattered, and mentally tired.

There's also a real toll on mental health. Heavy social media use is linked to higher rates of depression, anxiety, and loneliness (Neurolaunch, 2024). It's the constant comparisons, the "fear of missing out," the pressure to always appear a certain way online. All of this chips away at our emotional well-being, slowly and quietly, until we don't even notice how drained we feel.

Now, breaking an addiction isn't something you do on a whim. You don't just "try to cut down" and hope for the best. You have to decide, fully, that you're done feeding it. That you're willing to starve it, even when it screams for attention. Because until then, it owns you, your time, your mood, your focus, your sense of self.

With social media, you have to be intentional. It doesn't look dangerous. It's not a needle or a pill. It's in your pocket, in your bed, on your desk at work. You can justify it all day: "I'm just checking messages," "I'm learning things," "I'm relaxing."

You have to stop feeding the loop long enough for your brain to reset. Not just taking the phone away, but filling the gap with something that doesn't leave you emptier than you started. Here is how to start breaking free:

- Go cold turkey for short bursts. A few hours at first, then half a day, then longer. Let your brain feel the absence.
- Do something that holds your attention. Read, write, build, fix, draw, anything that forces you to stay with it.
- Catch the urge before you act on it. When your hand moves toward your phone, pause. Stand up, take a walk, or just do anything else but reach for the phone.
- Shut off the bait. No pings, no pop-ups, no vibrations.
- Feed your brain real rewards. Exercise, cook, play music, have actual face-to-face conversations.

Social Mirror Syndrome

A mirror is useful. Without it, you'd probably walk out with your shirt buttoned wrong or lipstick halfway across your cheek. It tells you the truth so you can fix yourself and move on.

Now imagine you're surrounded by a hundred mirrors. Not normal ones, warped ones. Some make you look better than you are, some worse, some just wrong. You don't get to pick which one you look into, but you start believing all of them anyway.

You see everyone else's "mirrors", perfect angles, perfect lighting, perfect smiles that probably cracked two seconds later. Even though you *know* it's staged, some part of you keeps measuring yourself against it. You start thinking, maybe I should look more like that. Maybe my life should feel more like that. Without realising, you start editing yourself. Posting only your best bits. Saying things that sound good, not things you really mean.

At first, it feels like nothing. Everyone filters themselves a little. You crop out the messy corner of your living room. You delete the video where you stumbled over your words. You share the photo where the light hit you just right. It's harmless, you tell yourself you're just putting your best foot forward. Yet, over time, you stop showing your real feet altogether. You replace them with the kind of feet you think will get applause.

It's easy to miss when the shift happens. One day you're living your life and occasionally documenting it; the next you're living in ways designed to be documented. You don't just go to a coffee shop, you go to the one with the aesthetic table by the window. You don't just take a walk, you find a wall with colourful street art to "accidentally" pass by. Somewhere in there, the mirror stops reflecting your life, and your life starts reflecting the mirror.

So, we learned to constantly scan for approval. We paid attention to the tone of voice, facial expressions, and the way people moved around us. We became experts in reading the "social mirror", the reflection of ourselves we could see in the eyes of others. This wasn't vanity. It was a survival skill burned into our brains over thousands of years.

The human brain wasn't built for this many reflections. It can't process them all, so it does something strange: it starts believing them all, even when they contradict each other. One mirror says you're too quiet; another says you're too loud. One says you're beautiful; another says you're plain. You try to fix both "problems" at once, and slowly, you sand down the edges of who you are until there's nothing sharp left.

Psychologists call the skill of adjusting yourself to fit the room "self-monitoring." In moderation, it's useful. It's how you know to lower your voice in a library or switch to a simpler language when talking to a child. However, when the self-monitoring never stops, when it becomes the default lens for every decision, something starts to rot. The performance replaces the person. You're no longer asking, Do I like this? You're asking, Will they like me like this?

The most dangerous part is how invisible the process feels from the inside. People rarely notice they're doing it until something forces them to go without their mirrors, a phone that dies, a week away from Wi-Fi, a friend who calls out the performance. That's when the anxiety hits. It's not just boredom or FOMO; it's the shaky, uncomfortable sense that you don't quite know who you are when no one is watching.

This syndrome shows up in more places than social media. It's in workplaces, where "professionalism" often means flattening yourself into something safe and inoffensive. It's in families, where you're cast in a role, the peacemaker, the funny one, the golden child, and expected to keep playing it long after it stops fitting. It's in friendships where you hide certain parts of yourself because you've learned they don't get a good reaction.

The effect can be slow and corrosive. Over time, your preferences stop feeling like yours. You might think you like a certain style of clothes, but really, you've learned that's the style that gets you compliments. You might think you enjoy a type of conversation, but really, you've learned that's what makes you seem interesting. Your desires start bending toward approval like plants twisting toward light, except here, the "light" is inconsistent, unreliable, and sometimes toxic.

The emotional cost is high. People living in this constant reflection loop often carry a low-level anxiety that never switches off. Even in private, there's a faint hum of self-consciousness, like someone might be watching. That mental "audience" becomes so ingrained that when it goes silent, it feels wrong. This is why taking a break from social media, for some people, doesn't feel restful, it feels like withdrawal.

It's tempting to think the solution is to smash all the mirrors. Quit social media. Stop caring what anyone thinks. However, the instinct to check your reflection isn't something you can delete. It's too old, too deeply woven into how humans survive together. The goal isn't to stop looking in mirrors; it's to learn which ones to trust, which ones to ignore, and how to see yourself without needing them at all.

The problem with modern mirrors isn't just their number; it's their distortion. Some are designed to make you feel worse so you'll buy something. Some are designed to make you feel better so you'll keep scrolling. Some are designed to show you what you already believe, even if it's untrue, so you won't leave the platform. You can't fix the distortion in the mirror. You can only decide how much of yourself to give.

That's where most people get stuck, not in seeing the problem, but in acting like it matters. They'll admit social media is fake but still let it dictate how they feel about themselves. They'll laugh at the absurdity of influencer culture while quietly wondering if they should be more like the influencers. They'll criticise "highlight reels" while curating their own. This isn't hypocrisy so much as it is the pull of that ancient wiring: the part of your brain that still believes being liked keeps you alive.

Breaking the pull means testing what it's like to go unseen. Not forever, just enough to notice how much of your life depends on the reflection. Do something you enjoy and don't post about it. Tell a truth that doesn't make you look good. Wear something you like even if it photographs badly. At first, it will feel wrong, like walking into the world with mismatched socks. However, slowly, the noise starts to fade. You stop checking how you look in other people's eyes every five minutes. You start noticing how you look on your own.

You won't get rid of all the mirrors. Life needs some of them. They help you spot spinach in your teeth and warn you when you're crossing a line. However, there's a difference between glancing at a mirror to get your bearings and living in one. The first keeps you grounded. The second makes you forget you ever had a face without it.

Digital Overidentification

Your online identity isn't just the pictures you choose to post or the words you consciously share. It's also the invisible trail of clues you leave behind every time you interact with the internet. What sites you linger on, which posts you scroll past slowly, the exact time of day you log in, the type of music you replay three times in a row, all of it adds up to a profile that is *you*, whether you recognise it or not.

This is your "data-self", a composite version of you built out of billions of small interactions. You don't get to curate this self the way you curate your Instagram feed. You can't delete the moments where your mouse hovered over something you didn't click, or where you half-read a comment thread before moving on. The data-self exists independently of your conscious presentation, and in some ways it's *more* "real" to the systems that interact with you.

Here's the unsettling part: algorithms know the data-self better than you do. They may be able to predict what kind of content will hold your attention at 11:37 p.m., which products you're more likely to buy when you're tired, or which songs make you nostalgic enough to keep streaming for hours. While this was originally sold as "personalisation," what it really means is that there's a second version of you out there, one that can be nudged, shaped, and sold.

When you start to see yourself through that lens, your own identity gets outsourced. You begin to wonder if the algorithm knows you better than you know yourself. You notice that your feed "gets you" in a way people sometimes don't, and without meaning to, you take cues from the data-self about what to like, what to watch, even what to want. The mirror isn't just reflecting you anymore, it's training you.

Social Mirror Syndrome isn't only about your own reflection, it's also about the reflections you borrow from others. This is where parasocial overidentification comes in. A "parasocial" relationship is the one-sided connection you feel with someone you've never actually met, a YouTuber, a podcast host, a TikTok personality. You know their laugh, their mannerisms, the way they talk about their morning coffee, and you start to feel like you know them.

In moderation, parasocial bonds aren't inherently harmful. They can make the media more engaging, even comforting. The trouble starts when you don't just connect with an influencer, you start absorbing them. Their preferences become your preferences. Their moral stance becomes yours. You feel protective over them, even defensive, as if criticism of them is criticism of you. The boundary between their life and your own starts to blur.

Over time, this can lead to an odd form of identity grafting. You're not just admiring someone, you're running your self-image through their mirror. If they start wearing a certain brand, you feel an urge to do the same. If they make a big life change, you wonder if you should too. You might not even notice how much of your self-concept is borrowed until they disappear or change direction, and you're left scrambling to fill in the gaps.

This is one of the reasons influencer scandals can feel so personally upsetting to followers. It's not just disappointment in another person, it's a kind of identity whiplash. If part of who you are is built on someone else's curated self, any crack in their image becomes a crack in yours.

There is also something called digital hyperconnectivity, the always-on state of being connected to people, platforms, and information. This isn't just "checking your phone a lot"; it's living in a continuous loop where your actions, thoughts, and even moods are mediated by a network.

In this state, your life becomes constantly measurable. Every post has a number attached, likes, views, comments, shares. Every action can be tracked: how far you walked today, how many hours you slept, how many words you typed. This is self-quantification, and while it can be motivating in short bursts, it also subtly rewires your sense of value.

Instead of asking, *Did I enjoy that?* you start asking, *Did that perform well?* Instead of thinking, *I'm proud of this,* you think, *I hope the numbers reflect how proud I feel.* Over time, the numbers start to feel like the truth, and your unmeasured experiences start to feel invisible or less important.

This creates a feedback loop that deepens Social Mirror Syndrome. The mirror no longer just shows you a social image; it shows you a scoreboard, and because numbers are clean and undeniable in a way feelings are not, it's easy to believe the scoreboard is the most accurate reflection. If the numbers go up, you feel worth more. If they go down, you feel worth less.

The combination of these forces, the data-self, parasocial overidentification, and self-quantification, means that the modern social mirror is unlike anything humans have faced before. It's not just wanting to be liked by the tribe. It's managing multiple versions of yourself, each reflected back to you by systems you don't fully control, while measuring your worth in real time against people you'll never meet.

No wonder it's exhausting.

The "Better Me" Illusion

The grass is greener where you water it. That's the old saying, anyway, because the culture we live in has a different version: *The grass is greener somewhere else, if you could just work harder, track more, optimize more, hustle more, buy this planner, take this course, start waking up at 5 a.m., then you'd finally get there.*

In fact, you don't even have to peek over a neighbor's fence to see their grass. You open your phone, and there it is, highlighting reels of other people's lives, curated to look just right. Their careers, vacations, workouts, relationships, even their breakfasts are on display, perfectly lit and perfectly timed.

On the surface, it looks like ambition, discipline, and growth. Underneath, it can quietly become a treadmill that moves faster the harder you run.

The idea of becoming a better version of yourself sounds harmless, noble even, but the paradox is that chasing a "better me" can quietly replace contentment with a constant sense of inadequacy.

It's bad enough when your goals shift because of your own high standards. It's worse when they shift because of other people's standards, their promotions, their toned bodies, their perfectly decorated homes. Every time, you're reminded of someone who seems to be a step ahead. Even if you don't consciously think I need to beat them, your brain is quietly updating the benchmark for "enough."

In the last decade, optimization culture has become its own economy, apps that log your steps, diet trackers that grade your meals, productivity gurus who promise you'll get ten times more done, "morning routine" videos where people with perfect skin sip matcha before sunrise. It's intoxicating because it feels like progress. However, it often trades genuine satisfaction for a restless itch that never goes away.

You can see it in people who are always "working on themselves," yet somehow always exhausted, burnt out, and secretly convinced they're failing. The same system that sells hope, if you just do this, you'll finally be your best self, also keeps moving the finish line so you never stop chasing.

Two powerful cognitive biases supercharge this treadmill:

- **Illusory superiority:** Most people rate themselves as "above average" in intelligence, kindness, and skill. It's comforting but not always accurate. When improvement plans are built on this, you can end up pushing for unrealistic leaps because

you assume you're starting closer to the finish line than you really are.
- **Optimism bias:** We tend to believe we're less likely than others to fail, and more likely to succeed. This is why so many people think *this* diet, *this* course, or *this* productivity system will finally be the one that changes everything.

The twist is that these biases don't exist in isolation. They feed off something even more insidious: upward social comparison, the constant measuring of yourself against those you believe are doing better.

It's one of the most quietly addictive forces in modern life. You scroll through your feed and see someone announcing their promotion, or sharing photos from a holiday you could never afford. You tell yourself you're just "catching up" on what friends are up to, but in reality, your brain is logging the data: They're ahead. You're behind.

Upward comparison is tough because it doesn't just produce one emotional reaction, it produces two, and they're both forceful.

1. **Hope:** When you see someone achieve something, a part of you lights up. If they can do it, maybe you can too. It feels motivating, like a challenge you can rise to meet. This is why "success story" posts are so popular, they trigger that possibility mindset.
2. **Shame:** The darker side comes when the gap between where you are and where they are feels too wide. That initial spark of hope curdles into something heavier: Why am I not there yet? What's wrong with me? This shame is quiet but corrosive, it doesn't necessarily push you forward, it just keeps whispering that you're not enough.

The danger is that these emotions don't cancel each other out, they form a loop.

Hope makes you chase harder. Shame makes you double down. The harder you chase, the more you notice others who are still ahead. The more you notice them, the more you need the next hit of progress to feel okay.

In this age of social media, this loop spins faster than ever. You're not comparing yourself to the ten or twenty people you see in your everyday life, you're comparing yourself to thousands of carefully curated lives. Upward comparison rarely compares you to the *whole* person. You're comparing your reality, messy, flawed, unfiltered, to their best five percent.

That's like comparing your behind-the-scenes footage to someone else's final, edited movie. You're never going to win that comparison, yet your brain keeps playing it as if it's a fair game.

Here's where it gets even more dangerous: upward social comparison interacts with illusory superiority and optimism bias in a way that keeps the treadmill running. You believe you're capable of "catching up" (optimism bias), and you think you're closer to that level than you actually are (illusory superiority), so you set higher and higher expectations for yourself. Then, when you inevitably fall short, you double down, convinced you just need one more push.

Over time, you're not just chasing improvement, you're chasing the elimination of the gap between you and the people you look up to. A gap that, in reality, is mostly a mirage.

There's a subtle but important question hidden inside all this: *Better for who?*

Many so-called self-improvements aren't actually about becoming a fuller, truer version of yourself. They're about shaping yourself to fit an image you think will be more acceptable, more lovable, more marketable, more impressive. That might mean polishing your social media presence, adopting fashionable opinions, or even pretending to enjoy activities that "better people" are supposed to like.

If you see the "ideal" version of success enough times, you can start moulding yourself toward it without realizing you're doing it. You might tell yourself you're improving when in reality you're just becoming a more convincing imitation of someone else's highlight reel.

Left unchecked, the "Better Me" mindset can turn into self-manipulation. You stop listening to what you truly need, and start bending yourself to meet external expectations, whether those expectations come from society, your boss, your peers, or even your own internalized critic.

Comparison makes this worse by adding constant proof that you're "behind." Even when you've made progress, it's easy to discount it because someone else has gone further. That constant gap between where you are and where they seem to be is mentally exhausting.

Add toxic positivity to the mix, the pressure to "stay positive" no matter what, and you end up suppressing the very struggles you need to acknowledge in order to heal. Over time, this constant suppression paired with endless striving leads to burnout: mental,

The tragedy is that the "Better Me" illusion is built on a real, healthy impulse. Psychologists call it the self-expansion drive, the deep human desire to grow, learn, and increase our ability to handle life. This drive is what makes people explore, fall in love, take risks, and build new skills.

Growth itself is not the problem. The problem comes when growth is hijacked by external pressures, when it stops being about living more fully and starts being about performing more convincingly.

The grass *is* greener where you water it, but when you're caught in the "Better Me" illusion, you're not really watering your grass at all, you're constantly wandering the neighbourhood, peering over fences, comparing shades of green, and wondering why yours never looks good enough.

Chapter Summary

- Breaking an addiction isn't something you do on a whim. You don't just "try to cut down" and hope for the best. You have to decide, fully, that you're done feeding it. Decide that you're willing to starve it, even when it screams for attention
- The problem with social mirrors isn't just their number; it's their distortion. Some are designed to make you feel worse so you'll buy something. Some are designed to make you feel better so you'll keep scrolling. Some are designed to show you what you already believe, even if it's untrue, so you won't leave the platform. You can't fix the distortion in the mirror. You can only decide how much of yourself to give.
- The idea of becoming a better version of yourself sounds harmless and noble but the paradox is that chasing a "better me" can quietly replace contentment with a constant sense of inadequacy.

4

The Catastrophe Machine

The taste for worst-case scenarios reflects the need to master fear of what is felt to be uncontrollable. It also expresses an imaginative complicity with disaster.
—Susan Sontag

I've never met anyone who planned for the worst and claimed it made them happier. Safer, maybe, but never happier. The mental habit of playing out every bad turn doesn't really protect you from much. Most of the time, it just makes you tense before anything's even happened. You spend hours or days rehearsing problems you won't ever have to face.

Sure, there are moments when caution saves you. Double-checking the lock before bed. Looking both ways twice before crossing the street is smart, but that's not the same as living in constant preparation for the worst. That's in no way safety. That's carrying an emergency you don't actually have.

Worst-case thinking hijacks your attention and dumps it into situations that don't even exist. It pulls your attention away from what's happening now and dumps it into situations that don't even exist, and the trade-off is rarely worth it. You lose peace in the present to feel slightly more prepared for a future that never arrives.

Mental Time Travel Gone Wrong

Mental time travel is what your brain does when it jumps back into the past or leaps forward into the future. You can be standing in your kitchen making coffee, but in your head, you're back in last week's argument. Or you're already in tomorrow's meeting, running through how you'll answer a tough question.

It's one of the most useful skills the brain has. It lets you remember how something went wrong so you don't repeat it. It lets you run little simulations in your head. What if I leave earlier? What if I take a different route? What will I say if they bring that up? Those mental rehearsals are what help you show up on time, stay prepared, and avoid looking like you have no idea what's going on.

The same mental trick that you use to remember to grab your charger before a trip is the one you use to picture where you'll sit when you get to a restaurant. You can "visit" the future without moving an inch. It's practical. It's clever, and when it's working well, it's what keeps life running smoothly.

The problem is, your brain doesn't just run positive simulations. If it can imagine the best version of an event, it can also run the absolute worst version, in high definition, on repeat. That's where the trouble starts.

Mental time travel isn't a bad thing. In fact, when it's working the way it's supposed to, it's what makes life run much more smoothly. It's the reason you don't get to the store and realize you forgot your wallet. It's the reason you remember to bring a jacket because the weather app said it might rain.

You think of the questions your boss might ask, the points you would love to make, and the way you'd phrase them so they land well. Even something as small as checking the weather before a picnic is future thinking. You're jumping ahead in your mind to imagine sitting outside with friends, and then adjusting your plan if the forecast says rain. It's super useful.

So future thinking is not the enemy here. The problem isn't that your brain looks ahead, it's that sometimes it won't stop. It takes the same skill that helps you plan a menu or remember an umbrella and uses the skill to build ten different disaster scenarios you didn't ask for. That's when mental time travel starts working against you.

The same brain that helps you plan a grocery list can also run wild. It takes a simple task, say, sending an email, and imagines fifty ways it could blow up. You hit "send" in your head, and suddenly you're picturing being misunderstood, getting a harsh reply, or somehow ruining your reputation.

That's the shift from planning to catastrophizing. Planning means you're preparing for what's likely. Catastrophising is when you're bracing for what's worst. It's like your brain's prediction system has the volume turned up too high, and instead of scanning for helpful information, it's scanning for trouble.

The problem is, your body can't always tell the difference between an imagined disaster and a real one. When you picture yourself fumbling your words in a meeting or getting bad news from a doctor, your body reacts as if it's actually happening. Your heart starts beating faster, your muscles get tense, and your breathing gets shallow. You start living in a stress response that hasn't even been earned by reality.

The more vividly you imagine the problem, the more real it feels. You can make yourself sweat over a situation that doesn't exist, lose sleep over a conversation that never happened, or ruin a perfectly fine day because your brain built a movie of everything going wrong and you sat through the whole screening.

Overactive Prediction Circuitry

Most people call it "overthinking." In reality, it's your brain's prediction system that's working harder than it should.

The human brain isn't just a passive sponge soaking up the world around you. It's more like a prediction machine. It's always trying to guess what will happen next, using your past experiences and the information it's picking up at the moment. This is called "predictive coding."

Here's how it usually works: your brain makes a prediction, compares it to reality, and then updates its model if it got things wrong. That way you don't have to process every single piece of raw data from scratch. It's efficient.

When this system is balanced, it only ramps up when there's real uncertainty or a genuine threat. However, in overactive prediction circuitry, that balance breaks leading to a prediction error. This is when your brain's guess doesn't match reality. Normally, that's no big deal, your brain quietly adjusts and moves on.

If your brain has learned that prediction errors could mean danger, it treats every mismatch as a problem. This creates prediction-error sensitivity. The brain starts acting like uncertainty itself is a threat. Instead of waiting and seeing, it feels the need to simulate every possible outcome immediately.

That's why something small, like not knowing if a package will arrive on time, can get you into a chain of what-ifs.

When your mind wanders or daydreams, the default mode network (DMN) switches on. In a healthy rhythm, the DMN turns on when you're at rest and turns down when you need to focus. With overactive prediction circuitry, it flips on too often and stays on too long. This makes your mind drift into future-simulating mode, even when you want to stay present.

The more it runs, the stronger those pathways get. Over time, prediction mode becomes the brain's default habit.

Another piece is the salience network, which decides what deserves your attention. Think of it as your brain's filter. Normally, it passes along only the signals that really matter.

In overactive prediction circuitry, this filter becomes overzealous. It tags more and more things as "important," which means your prediction machinery has to process a larger load. That's why it can feel like everything is urgent or needs to be thought through in detail.

Put all this together: a jumpy amygdala, an overactive default mode network, a salience filter that tags too much, and a brain that treats uncertainty like danger, and you get a mind that rarely rests.

The predictions it makes aren't evenly balanced either. Because of negativity bias, the brain pays more attention to threats than to neutral or positive possibilities. That's why imagined disasters tend to dominate over imagined successes. Even when you picture a good outcome, it's usually followed by "yes, but what if…" This results in:

- Attention getting scattered. Your focus is split between the present and the endless "what ifs," which ironically makes mistakes more likely.
- The body is carrying stress. Imagining stressful situations can trigger physical reactions: faster heartbeat, tense muscles, shallow breathing, stress hormones. Multiply that by dozens of scenarios a day and your body never really comes down from alert mode.
- Decision-making slows. Too many possible futures to weigh leads to analysis paralysis. Choices get delayed, or avoided altogether. Sometimes opportunities are missed simply because the brain was too busy simulating.
- Avoidance becomes tempting. To reduce the flood of scenarios, people may skip events, stick to routines, or decline opportunities. It feels safer than feeding the overprediction loop.

The brain strengthens the pathways it uses the most. So the more you overpredict, the easier it becomes to keep doing it. If you predicted something bad and it didn't happen, your brain might decide the prediction itself prevented it. That false conclusion teaches your brain to keep running predictions, even though it had nothing to do with the outcome.

The Safety Illusion

Most of us like to think that safety is something you can lock down if you just work hard enough. The right decisions, enough preparation, the right people around you, it can feel like there's a formula. If you follow it, you should be able to stay out of harm's way.

That belief is comforting. It makes life feel more predictable. The problem is, a lot of what we think of as "safety" is an illusion created by the brain to calm itself down. It's not that there's no such thing as safety, but the version we picture, complete control, zero uncertainty, doesn't exist.

Your brain likes certainty. It treats it almost like a basic need. Uncertainty feels like standing on a shaky bridge, so the brain starts looking for ways to make the bridge feel solid, even if the planks underneath aren't actually stronger. It builds patterns, routines, and "rules" about what is safe and what isn't. Maybe you only feel comfortable driving a certain route, or you avoid certain situations because you've convinced yourself they're unsafe. These patterns give you a sense of control, but they also quietly shrink your life.

This illusion can be especially strong if you've experienced a painful shock or sudden loss in the past. Something bad happened once, so your brain decides it needs to be on guard all the time. It creates rituals, habits, and "safety checks" to make sure it never happens again.

These checks can be as small as triple-checking you locked the door, or as big as avoiding travel altogether. Over time, you stop noticing that you're building your life around avoiding discomfort rather than living fully.

The hardest part is that these strategies work, but only to a point. They can keep you out of immediate trouble, but they can't erase uncertainty from life. The sense of security they give you is temporary.

As soon as one risk is removed, your brain will find another one to worry about. You start chasing safety like it's something you can store up, but the tank never seems full. The moment you feel secure, your brain is already scanning for the next possible danger.

The safety illusion can also trick you into thinking you're protecting yourself when you're actually making yourself more anxious. For example, constantly checking the news to "stay informed" might give you a brief sense of control, but it keeps your mind in a loop of looking for threats.

Avoiding certain social situations because they make you nervous might calm you in the moment, but it reinforces the belief that those situations are dangerous. Each time you give in to the illusion, the brain learns, *This works,* and the pattern gets stronger.

The truth is, real safety comes from flexibility, not from locking down every variable. You don't have to eliminate uncertainty but know you can handle what comes. The brain's illusion of safety tells you that the only way to feel secure is to remove all possible risks, something no one can do.

Letting go of that idea can feel terrifying at first, because it means admitting you can't control everything, but once you see that the illusion isn't keeping you as safe as you thought, you can start building a different kind of security, one based on skills, resilience, and the ability to recover from setbacks rather than avoid them entirely.

The safety illusion doesn't just limit your life, it feeds anxiety in a way that can make it feel impossible to break free. At first, the patterns you build around safety seem harmless, even smart.

Anxiety thrives on this loop. You feel unsafe, so you try to control or avoid the situation. The avoidance gives you a brief sense of safety. Your brain takes note: *Good, we dodged danger.* That reinforces the idea that the danger was real and that avoidance is the only thing keeping you safe.

The next time you're in a similar situation, the anxiety comes back even faster, because your brain has learned to expect it. Over weeks or years, this can turn into a long list of "off-limits" situations, until even small things start feeling risky.

This is where the safety illusion gets particularly cruel. It convinces you that the only reason nothing bad has happened is because you've been careful enough. So you stay careful, more careful than before, adding new precautions to your life. This might mean carrying extra items "just in case," spending hours researching every possible risk before making a decision, or avoiding certain people because you're afraid of what they might say or do. The more precautions you add, the more you believe you need them. It becomes exhausting.

Physically, your body isn't designed to stay in a state of constant alert. When you live inside the safety illusion, your nervous system is always half-braced for impact, even when nothing is happening. Your muscles stay tense, your heart rate stays slightly elevated, your breathing is shallower. This low-grade stress might not feel as dramatic as a full-blown panic attack, but over time it wears you down. It makes concentration harder, sleep less restful, and small frustrations more overwhelming.

Mentally, the safety illusion robs you of the ability to trust yourself. When you believe safety only comes from controlling the outside world, you never get the chance to see how you can cope when things go wrong. You don't build evidence that you can handle uncertainty, because you never let yourself experience it. That means every unknown stays scary. Even neutral situations, a last-minute change of plans, a new task at work, an unexpected phone call, can trigger the same tight, anxious feeling in your chest.

Breaking this cycle means you have to slowly teach your brain that safety can exist even when things aren't certain. That means, sometimes, choosing not to check again, not to plan for every possible outcome, and not to avoid the situations that make you slightly uncomfortable. Each time you do that, you give your brain proof that uncertainty is survivable. Over time, that proof builds real confidence, the kind that doesn't depend on the illusion of total control.

Why Certainty Feels Safer Than Joy

When you've lived with anxiety, you learn to scan ahead, to predict outcomes, to keep things as controlled as possible. Over time, certainty starts to feel like safety. It doesn't matter whether that certainty makes you happy, it just matters that it feels predictable.

That's why people so often choose the familiar discomfort over the unfamiliar possibility of joy. A bad job you know is still more familiar than risking a new one that might fail. A relationship that feels flat but stable is easier to stay in than opening yourself up to someone new. The brain sees the stability of the current situation and thinks, *At least I know what I'm dealing with.*

From a nervous system perspective, this makes sense. The body prefers patterns. When it can predict what's going to happen next, it can relax, even if "relax" just means settling into a low-grade stress that never changes. It's a bit like living next to a noisy road. The sound isn't pleasant, but eventually, your brain tunes it out. Move to a new place where it's quiet, and suddenly you notice every little creak in the floorboards.

That's what joy can feel like to someone used to bracing for bad news, strange, foreign, even suspicious. Your brain isn't used to the high, so it waits for the drop. It treats happiness as a warning sign: *If things are good now, something bad is coming.* That fear is enough to push many people back into predictable routines, where there's less to lose.

The trouble is, living for certainty comes with a hidden cost. You start avoiding the situations that carry risk, which also happen to be the situations most likely to bring joy. You choose the safe option, not because it's the best, but because it's the one you can imagine from start to finish without surprise.

The logic is simple: *If I don't get my hopes up, I won't get hurt.* The reality is harsher: you shrink your world. You stop trying new things, meeting new people, or taking on challenges that matter to you. Life becomes smaller, not safer, just smaller.

And here's the thing certainty won't tell you: it's not actually certain. Jobs end. Relationships change. Health shifts overnight. No matter how much you plan or avoid, life will still throw curveballs. The certainty you're clinging to is temporary, but the opportunities you turn down because of it? Those can be gone for good.

Let me show you what this looks like in everyday life:

- **Work:** You stay in a role you've outgrown because you know the routines and personalities. A new job could be better, but it also means interviews, probation periods, and the risk of failing.
- **Relationships:** You keep investing in a friendship that drains you because starting over with new people feels too uncertain.
- **Life choices:** You avoid traveling somewhere you've always wanted to go because you're worried about what might go wrong, even if the chances are small.

In each case, the "safe" choice isn't actually safe. It just *feels* safer because the outcomes are familiar.

Here's the real problem: certainty and joy rarely live in the same place. Joy, by nature, comes with some uncertainty. You don't know if the new person you meet will become a lifelong friend or just a passing acquaintance. You can't guarantee that the project you're excited about will succeed. You can't promise yourself that the trip will go exactly as planned.

If you're committed to only making moves where the outcome is guaranteed, you're also committing to skipping most of the things that make life worth living.

The way out isn't to eliminate your desire for stability. Stability has its place. The goal is to make uncertainty less threatening so you can actually choose joy when it's available.

1. **Start Small:** Don't leap straight into life-changing risks. Practice with low-stakes uncertainty: try a new restaurant without checking reviews, start a hobby without knowing if you'll be good at it, join a group where you don't know anyone.
2. **Notice Your Body's Reaction:** When you feel the urge to retreat to certainty, pay attention to what's happening physically, tightness in the chest, faster breathing, tension in the shoulders. Recognising it makes it easier to ride it out.
3. **Separate Discomfort from Danger:** Your brain might treat uncertainty as danger, but they're not the same. Remind yourself: "I'm uncomfortable, but I'm not unsafe."
4. **Anchor to Your Values, Not Outcomes:** If your decision is based on what matters to you, you can tolerate a wider range of possible outcomes. Even if it doesn't go perfectly, you acted in alignment with your values.
5. **Collect Evidence You Can Cope:** Keep track of times you faced uncertainty and it worked out, or when it didn't work out but you

handled it anyway. Your brain needs reminders that you can survive the unknown.

The more you expose yourself to uncertainty in manageable doses, the more you shift your focus from needing control to trusting your ability to cope. You stop demanding guarantees and start building confidence in yourself. Not confidence that everything will go right, but confidence that you'll be okay even if it doesn't.

That kind of trust is worth more than certainty. Certainty can vanish in a moment; trust in yourself stays with you. And when you have it, you don't have to choose between safety and joy, you can carry both into the same room and know you can handle whatever happens next.

Hypervigilance as a Survival Strategy

Hypervigilance is the state of being constantly alert, scanning for potential threats, even when there is no immediate danger. I like to describe it as having your "internal alarm system" stuck in the on position. While this heightened state of awareness can be a protective response in genuinely unsafe situations, it can become exhausting and counterproductive when it persists long after the danger has passed.

In healthy doses, vigilance is a normal part of human functioning. It helps you notice when something in your environment changes, detect subtle cues that something might be wrong, and respond quickly when needed.

For example, when you're crossing a busy street, you need to be alert to oncoming traffic, unpredictable drivers, and environmental obstacles. In situations like these, vigilance is adaptive, it keeps you alive and safe.

However, hypervigilance goes beyond adaptive alertness. In this state, the brain and body remain on constant high alert, monitoring for signs of trouble in every environment, even safe ones. People experiencing hypervigilance would find it difficult to relax, struggle to focus on anything beyond scanning for potential threats, and can misinterpret neutral cues, such as a stranger's facial expression, as signs of danger. Over time, this heightened sensitivity can distort perception, making the world feel more dangerous than it truly is.

One reason hypervigilance is so persistent is that it is closely linked to the body's stress response. When the brain's amygdala is overactive, it sends frequent signals to the hypothalamus to trigger the fight-or-flight system.

This floods the body with stress hormones like cortisol and adrenaline. These chemicals sharpen your senses and prepare you to act quickly, but if they remain elevated for too long, they can cause fatigue, irritability, muscle tension, headaches, and trouble sleeping. The body is not designed to stay in this heightened state indefinitely.

Research has shown that hypervigilance is common in people who have experienced trauma. For example, individuals with post-traumatic stress disorder (PTSD) tend to remain on high alert because their brains have learned to associate certain environments or cues with past danger (van der Kolk, 2014). Even when the current environment is safe, the nervous system can react as if the threat is still present. You're not just "overthinking", it is actually a deeply ingrained survival adaptation that the brain has difficulty turning off.

Hypervigilance is not only connected to trauma. It also shows up in conditions like generalized anxiety disorder (GAD), obsessive-compulsive disorder (OCD), and some personality disorders. The common thread is that the person's mind is always on alert, constantly scanning for threats. Sometimes it's because of chronic worry, sometimes because of a fear of uncertainty, or even perfectionistic tendencies.

No matter the cause, the underlying mechanism is the same: the brain convinces itself that being on guard will prevent bad things from happening. On the surface, this seems protective. The logic goes, if I stay alert, I won't be caught off guard. However, it rarely works that way. What really happens is that your attention becomes narrowed and consumed by what might go wrong. In the process, you miss out on the things that could go right. Opportunities, joy, and moments of connection often slip by unnoticed because your energy is tied up in anticipating threats.

Living in constant hypervigilance takes a toll in almost every area of life. At work, it can make you second-guess your decisions, overcheck your tasks, or hesitate to take on new challenges because you're too focused on possible mistakes.

In relationships, it can create tension, your partner, friends, or colleagues might feel that you're always on edge or hard to relax around.

In fact, parenting under hypervigilance can mean being overly controlling or reactive, which makes it difficult to enjoy time with your children or to give them space to grow. On a personal level, hypervigilance drains energy, fuels fatigue, and keeps you from experiencing the simple ease that makes life feel balanced and meaningful.

Overgeneralisation and the Danger of "Always" and "Never" Thinking

It feels safe to put life into neat categories: good or bad, success or failure, right or wrong. It's easier for the mind to say, "This is always true" or "That will never happen" than to hold onto complexity. Yet life rarely fits so neatly into black and white boxes. More often than not, it's grey. Two truths, or even more, can exist at the same time, and learning to sit with that complexity is one of the most important skills for emotional balance.

Think about how we talk about people. Someone can be caring and still make selfish decisions. A friend can deeply love you but also disappoint you sometimes. A parent might have caused pain and still have done their best with what they knew at the time.

These statements may seem contradictory, but they can all be true together. Accepting this duality is difficult because the brain wants one clear answer, it wants to know whether someone is safe or unsafe, good or bad. Yet real life does not offer such simple clarity.

When we deny the coexistence of multiple truths, we slide into overgeneralisation. For instance, one failure at work becomes "I'm terrible at my job." A painful breakup becomes "I'll never find love." The nuance disappears, and what was once a specific situation now defines the whole of reality.

The grey space is where growth happens. It's the recognition that "I failed at this project" can sit alongside "I am still capable." Or "That relationship hurt me deeply" can exist with "Love is still possible." Holding these layered truths does not erase pain; instead, it prevents pain from becoming the whole story.

Living in the grey also helps us stay open. It allows us to acknowledge what has gone wrong without shutting the door on what could go right. For example, you can admit that your anxiety makes social situations hard while also recognizing that you still crave connection and joy. You can honor both parts of your reality without choosing one over the other.

This flexibility is essential because rigid thinking, while comforting in its simplicity, rarely reflects reality. Life is contradictory. Joy can coexist with grief. Success can exist alongside self-doubt. Strength can be found in vulnerability. The more we allow space for these tensions, the more resilient we become.

I met Ella in her early thirties, around the time she finally left her first husband. On the surface, he had looked like everything she thought she wanted, confident, successful, well-spoken. Beneath that polished exterior was a narcissist who thrived on control.

Over the years, he made her second-guess herself at every turn. If she expressed sadness, he called her dramatic. If she questioned him, he accused her of being ungrateful. Slowly, he chipped away at her sense of self until Ella hardly recognized the woman staring back at her in the mirror.

When she finally found the strength to leave, Ella carried more than just scars. She carried a belief that became her shield: *"All men are the same."* It felt like protection. If she convinced herself that every man was like her ex, then she could avoid the pain of being fooled again. The logic was simple, better to be cautious and alone than open herself up to betrayal.

So when someone new approached her, she barely gave them a chance. She would scrutinize their words, searching for signs of manipulation. She would dismiss kindness as strategy and distance herself the moment she felt too seen. On dating apps, she swiped past dozens of men without even considering a conversation.

This belief became a filter that shaped every interaction. Even when she met genuinely kind men, friends of friends who asked her out respectfully, Ella's guard was always up. She would smile politely but decline, telling herself she was simply being smart. What she didn't see was how this shield was quietly stealing opportunities for love, companionship, and healing.

In the process, Ella lost years of potential connection. She missed dinners that could have turned into friendships, conversations that could have opened doors, and small acts of care that might have softened her wounds. Her overgeneralisation, the belief that her ex-husband's cruelty defined every man, kept her in a cycle of isolation.

Overgeneralisation is one of the most common mental traps. First, it distorts reality. Overgeneralisation removes nuance. If you fail one exam, the thought "I'm a failure" erases every past success. If one person betrays you, the belief "No one can be trusted" blocks you from seeing those who are genuinely loyal. Instead of holding both truths, the pain and the possibility, the mind clings to the negative one and applies it everywhere. This narrowing of perspective prevents you from seeing the full picture.

Second, it limits opportunities. When you believe *"I always mess things up"* or *"This never works out,"* you become hesitant to try again. New experiences feel pointless because the outcome already seems written. This creates a self-fulfilling cycle: by expecting failure, you avoid risks, and by avoiding risks, you never give yourself the chance to succeed. Over time, your world becomes smaller.

Third, overgeneralisation damages relationships. When you approach others with the assumption that they will hurt you, disappoint you, or betray you, it affects how you interact with them. You may keep your guard so high that no one can get close. Or you may interpret neutral behavior as negative because you're primed to expect the worst. The result is distance, mistrust, and loneliness.

Fourth, it erodes self-worth. Overgeneralisation turns inward. One mistake can become evidence that you are incapable. One rejection can convince you that you are unlovable. These absolute judgments feel final, as if one event has defined your entire identity. Carrying this belief weighs heavily on mental health, feeding anxiety and depression.

Overgeneralisation steals joy from the present. When your attention is fixed on "always" and "never," you are less able to notice small wins, moments of kindness, or signs of progress. You become so focused on protecting yourself from future disappointment that you overlook what is going right in the here and now.

The real danger of overgeneralisation is not just that it misrepresents reality, it also robs you of possibilities. By locking you into rigid rules, it keeps you from seeing that life is layered, unpredictable, and capable of surprising you in good ways too.

Escaping this trap requires slowing down and questioning your absolutes. Instead of "I always fail," ask, "When have I succeeded?" Instead of "People never stay," ask, "Who has been there for me?" These questions don't deny your pain; they simply open space for more truths to exist. And when more truths exist, so do more paths forward.

Chapter Summary

- The human brain isn't just a passive sponge soaking up the world around you. It's more like a prediction machine. It's always trying to guess what will happen next, using your past experiences and the information it's picking up at the moment. This is called "predictive coding."
- Your brain likes certainty. It treats it almost like a basic need. Uncertainty feels like standing on a shaky bridge, so the brain starts looking for ways to make the bridge feel solid, even if the planks underneath aren't actually stronger. It builds patterns, routines, and "rules" about what is safe and what isn't.

- When you've lived with anxiety, you learn to scan ahead, to predict outcomes, to keep things as controlled as possible. Over time, certainty starts to feel like safety. It doesn't matter whether that certainty makes you happy, it just matters that it feels predictable.

PART 2

The Science of Change

Change doesn't crash into your life by accident. It's not a burst of luck or a rare personality trait. Change can be explained. It has patterns, formulas, methods. Your brain runs on systems, chemistry, wiring, memory, belief, and those systems can be rewired.

This is where we lift the hood and watch the machinery move.

Where you see why thoughts feel heavier than they are. Why belief can shift biology. Why memories rewrite themselves. Why fake positivity backfires every time.

Change isn't mystery. It's mechanics.

And once you understand the science, you can use it on purpose.

PART 2

The Science of Change

5

Thoughts Are Just Chemicals

> Thoughts are chemical. They can either kill us or cure us.
> —Bernie Siegel

In 1921, an Austrian scientist named Otto Loewi had a dream that wouldn't leave him alone. He had spent years wrestling with a question that split the scientific world at the time: how exactly do nerves send signals? Was it just tiny bursts of electricity, or was there some kind of chemical messenger involved? No one could prove it either way.

That night, Loewi dreamed of an experiment with two frog hearts. In the dream, the setup was simple: keep both hearts alive in a salty solution, stimulate a nerve on one of them, and then see if anything transferred through the fluid to the other. He woke up convinced he'd seen the answer. By morning, the idea had slipped away. The next night, the dream came back, and this time he didn't wait. He went straight to his lab and set it up exactly as he'd seen it.

He stimulated the vagus nerve on the first frog heart, which predictably slowed its beating. Then he took some of the fluid from that heart and applied it to the second. To his shock, the second heart also slowed down, even though no nerve had been touched. Something in the fluid had carried the signal.

Loewi called it Vagusstoff, "the vagus substance." Later, scientists identified it as acetylcholine, the very first neurotransmitter ever discovered. With that, Loewi had proven that nerves don't just fire electricity like wires. They release chemicals that carry messages.

This was more than a neat trick with frogs. It cracked open an entirely new way of understanding the brain. If chemicals could carry signals that slowed a heartbeat, then chemicals could also shape moods, trigger memories, fuel motivation, or sink someone into despair. Every thought, every shift in emotion, every flash of fear or joy was tied to these invisible messengers.

Over the decades, researchers uncovered more of them: dopamine, serotonin, norepinephrine, GABA, glutamate, cortisol, oxytocin, each with its own role in how we feel and act. Some made us alert, some calmed us down, some lifted our mood, some dragged it under. They were like keys on a keyboard, pressing out the music of our inner life.

That discovery flipped everything. Thoughts weren't some untouchable mystery anymore, they had weight, substance, cause and effect. They weren't permanent truths, they were chemical events. Which means they can shift. They can be influenced. They can go wrong, and they can be put right again.

The next question is obvious: if thoughts are chemicals, then what is a thought, really?

What is a Thought, Really?

Most of us go through life assuming thoughts are like little sentences or pictures in the head. That's what it feels like. You "hear" your inner voice, you "see" an image in your mind, and you call that a thought. However, if you peel back the surface, what's happening underneath is both stranger and more precise.

At the most basic level, a thought begins as an electrical impulse. Your brain contains about 86 billion neurons. Each neuron can connect to thousands of others, creating trillions of possible connections. These connections form circuits and networks, kind of like overlapping highways of information.

One of the biggest myths about thoughts is that they are facts. If you think, *"I'm worthless,"* it doesn't just feel like an idea, it feels like reality. However, a thought, no matter how convincing, is not proof. It's a mental event influenced by mood, memory, or fear. Still, because the brain is wired to believe its own stories, it's easy to treat them like absolute truth.

Another myth is the idea that you can control all your thoughts. The reality is, most thoughts appear without your permission. The brain produces thousands every day, like clouds drifting across the sky. Some make sense, some are intrusive, and some vanish before you even notice them. Trying to control them all is impossible.

There's also the fear that having a bad thought makes you a bad person. It doesn't. The brain can spit out random, unwanted images or ideas. What matters is not the thought itself but what you do with it. Everyone has dark or strange thoughts at some point. That's just how the mind works.

Then there's the belief that if you think something enough, it becomes reality. Thoughts are powerful, yes, but not magical. You don't literally become your thoughts. A thought like *"I'm a failure"* is not the same as you actually being a failure. It's just an idea your brain is throwing at you. If you believe that thought over and over, and then start living as if it's true, it can end up shaping your life in ways that make it feel real.

Think about it this way: if you keep telling yourself you'll never succeed, chances are you'll stop trying new things. You hesitate to take risks or give up halfway through because the thought has already convinced you that the effort won't matter. Over time, those choices create a pattern of missed opportunities. Eventually, the thought that started in your mind becomes reflected in your life.

This is how thoughts influence reality, not by magic, but by guiding behavior. The opposite is also true. If you repeatedly tell yourself, *"I can figure this out,"* you're more likely to persevere and look for solutions. The thought doesn't guarantee success, but it changes how you show up, which increases the chances.

So no, you are not your thoughts, but if you let them go unchecked, they can become self-fulfilling. That's why awareness is so important. When you pause and say, *"This is just a thought, not a fact,"* you break the cycle. You get to choose whether to act on it or not.

Thoughts are powerful, but maybe not in the way people often assume. They don't bend reality just by existing. Their power lies in how they shape your emotions, your decisions, and even your body's reactions.

They also shape perception. If you wake up convinced that today will be a disaster, your brain will scan for evidence to prove it right. You'll notice every traffic jam, every sigh from your boss, every small mistake. On the other hand, if you wake up telling yourself, *"Today might be tough, but I can handle it,"* your brain tunes into resources and solutions. The day itself may not change, but the experience of it will.

Over time, repeated thoughts carve patterns in the brain. This is neuroplasticity. The more you think along a certain path, whether negative or balanced, the stronger that pathway becomes, making similar thoughts easier to access next time. This is why people stuck in cycles of worry or self-criticism often find it so hard to break free. The brain has literally been wired to default that way.

Thoughts move quickly, often slipping past unnoticed, but with awareness, you can catch them in the act.

Catching a thought means pausing long enough to recognize it. Maybe you feel a wave of anxiety before a meeting. If you stop and ask, *"What was I just thinking?"* you realize it was, *"I'm going to embarrass myself."* That recognition alone is a lot, because it stops the thought from hiding in the background and silently running the show.

Once you catch a thought, you can examine it. Is it a fact, or is it just a prediction? What evidence supports it? What evidence goes against it? How would you respond if a close friend had the same thought? Questions like these weaken the grip of negative thinking.

The brain is adaptable. Longstanding thought habits don't change overnight, but with repetition, new pathways form. Over time, balanced thinking can become the default, and unhelpful thoughts lose their authority.

So yes, you can catch your thoughts. You can challenge them, soften them, and replace them with something more balanced. You may not control what shows up in your mind, but you always have a choice about what to do next.

Serotonin, Dopamine, Cortisol

Thoughts don't just appear out of nowhere. They're shaped by a mix of things, biology, environment, and experience all leave their fingerprints.

Let's start with biology. The brain is an organ, and like any organ, it depends on chemistry, blood flow, sleep, and nutrition. A tired brain, for instance, is far more likely to slip into negative or repetitive thoughts. Lack of sleep doesn't just make you yawn, it changes how your prefrontal cortex regulates emotions, which means anxious or intrusive thoughts come easier.

Environment also matters. If you live in constant stress, say, in an unsafe home, a demanding workplace, or a relationship full of tension, your brain learns to prioritize survival over calm reflection. It leans toward scanning for danger rather than daydreaming about possibilities. Over time, the environment can literally "train" the brain to expect certain outcomes.

Then there's experience. Past trauma, patterns you grew up with, and even repeated stories you've told yourself become templates your brain uses to predict the future. If every time you spoke up as a child you were shut down, your adult brain may automatically generate thoughts like, "No one wants to hear me." Not because it's true now, but because that was the pattern then.

Culture, too, seeps in. The values you're surrounded by, whether achievement-focused, family-oriented, or survival-driven, help frame what kinds of thoughts feel natural or believable.

So, our thoughts aren't just personal creations. They're constantly being shaped by the state of our body, the chemicals flowing in our brain, the environment we're in, the experiences we've lived through, and the cultural air we breathe. Knowing this can loosen the grip of self-blame. It's not that you're weak for thinking a certain way, it's that your brain is responding to forces both inside and outside of you.

One of the biggest internal forces is chemistry. The brain is always awash in signals that influence what kind of thoughts show up and how strongly they take hold. That's why when people talk about the brain, chemicals like serotonin, dopamine, and cortisol often come up. They're not the whole picture, but they play a massive role in how thoughts are colored, how they rise, and how sticky they become.

Serotonin is usually referred to as the "feel good" chemical, but that's not quite accurate. It doesn't make you euphoric. It's more like an anchor, it keeps your mood steady, your thoughts balanced, and your emotional responses from swinging too far in one direction.

When serotonin levels are healthy, your thoughts have space. You're able to notice a difficult thought like, "I'm not good enough at this job," without collapsing into despair. It doesn't erase hard thoughts, but it gives you the ability to hold them lightly, to see them in context rather than as absolute truths.

When serotonin dips, though, thoughts turn heavy. They feel darker, harder to question, and more repetitive. This is one reason low serotonin is linked with depression. It's not that people suddenly become more "negative," it's that their brain chemistry makes it harder to lift thoughts out of the mud. The lens darkens, and every thought gets tinted.

Sleep, diet, sunlight, and even gut health affect serotonin. That's why a few days of poor rest or being stuck indoors can make your mind feel heavier than usual.

Dopamine is the motivator. It's tied to reward, anticipation, and the sense that something is worth chasing. Every time you think, "If I do this, something good might come," dopamine is involved.

Healthy dopamine levels help your thoughts lean forward. They make you curious, willing to plan, able to imagine better outcomes. When dopamine is flowing, the brain says, "This effort is worth it." You're able to connect the thought in your head to an action in the world.

When dopamine is low, thoughts feel flat. They might still be there, but they lack energy. You can think about goals, imagine possibilities, even recognize opportunities, but without dopamine, those thoughts don't fuel action. They sit in the corner, gathering dust. That's why low dopamine is linked to apathy and low motivation.

Dopamine is also involved in habits and addiction. The brain learns to release dopamine when you anticipate certain rewards, scrolling social media, eating sugar, taking risks. Over time, your thoughts can get pulled toward those rewards, sometimes at the expense of long-term goals. It's not weakness, it's the chemistry of anticipation.

Cortisol is your stress hormone. It's released when the brain detects danger, and its job is to keep you alive. Short bursts of cortisol sharpen your attention, quicken your reactions, and get you ready to respond. In real danger, it's lifesaving.

The problem is when cortisol stays elevated for too long. A brain marinated in cortisol is a brain on edge. Thoughts tilt toward scanning for threats, rehearsing worst-case scenarios, and magnifying small problems into big ones. Even when nothing is happening, your mind acts like it's already in crisis.

Over time, this state of hyper-alertness reshapes thought patterns. You start to expect disaster, doubt safety, and find it harder to relax. Your brain learns to equate calm with danger, because every time you try to slow down, cortisol whispers, "What if you're not ready when something happens?"

Chronic stress, then, isn't just a feeling, it literally sculpts your thinking. It makes you believe your anxious thoughts are realistic, even when they're not.

These chemicals don't work in isolation. They constantly push and pull on one another.

Too much cortisol, for instance, suppresses serotonin. That's why chronic stress so often leads to low mood, your stabilizer is being weakened by your alarm system. At the same time, high cortisol reduces dopamine, which explains why stress can make you feel both anxious and unmotivated.

On the other hand, balanced serotonin supports dopamine function, giving you both stability and drive. That's when thoughts feel both steady and energized, you're not just surviving, you're able to imagine, plan, and act.

Imagine waking up after a full night of rest, sunlight streaming in. Your serotonin is topped up, dopamine is waiting for cues, cortisol is low because you feel safe. Thoughts in this state are often clearer, more flexible, more hopeful.

Now imagine waking up after three nights of poor sleep, with work stress heavy on your shoulders. Cortisol is already high before you even get out of bed. Your serotonin is drained, your dopamine is sluggish. The thoughts that pop up are colored differently: "I can't do this," "Everything will go wrong," "What's the point?" They feel true, not because they are, but because your chemistry is skewed.

This doesn't mean your brain chemicals completely control you. They don't write the script of your life. What they do is set the stage, tilt the lighting, and influence the tone. Thoughts emerge inside this chemistry, and knowing that helps you see them more clearly. Sometimes what feels like "truth" is just cortisol shouting, or low dopamine making you feel defeated.

Neurotransmitter Loops and Self-Sabotage

Self-sabotage is when you end up working against yourself, even though you want something different. Your actions, or sometimes your lack of action, block the very goals you care about. You want a stable relationship, but you keep pulling away or starting fights. You want to save money, but you find yourself spending it the moment it comes in.

You want to finish a project, but you keep putting it off until you're scrambling at the last minute. Naturally, it feels confusing, almost like you're standing in your own way for no reason. Deep down, though, self-sabotage usually comes from patterns your brain and body have learned over time.

There isn't just one cause. Usually, self-sabotage starts with fear, fear of failure, fear of rejection, fear of losing control. For example, if you grew up in an environment where mistakes were punished harshly, you avoid challenges now, because your brain links risk with danger.

If you've been abandoned before, you can pull away from closeness today, because your body remembers how painful loss felt. Even if your current situation is safer, your nervous system doesn't always update.

Another cause is stress chemistry. High cortisol keeps your body on alert, making it harder to take calm, thoughtful steps forward. Low dopamine makes it harder to feel motivated, so tasks that matter feel empty. Low serotonin can make you impatient or irritable, so small problems feel overwhelming. These shifts aren't a reflection of who you are as a person, they're just brain states that shape behavior.

There's also the role of learned habits. If, for years, you've coped with anxiety by avoiding things, avoidance itself becomes automatic. If you've numbed pain with food, alcohol, or endless scrolling, your brain wires those actions into its "relief system." Over time, those habits turn into patterns that look like self-sabotage.

Is self-sabotage your fault? The short answer is no, self-sabotage is not simply your fault. Most of the time, the behaviors you call sabotage started as survival strategies. They protected you once, or at least made life feel safer. If you avoided, lashed out, overworked, or numbed yourself, it was likely because, in that moment of your past, it helped you get through. The problem is that those old protective patterns don't always let go on their own. They keep showing up, even when they're no longer useful.

That said, while it's not your fault, it does become your responsibility, in the sense that you're the only one who can begin to notice these patterns and slowly retrain your brain to respond differently.

You didn't choose to carry these habits, but you can choose how to move forward with them. Healing doesn't mean blaming yourself; it means understanding why these behaviors exist, and then teaching your nervous system safer, healthier ways to respond.

I'll map some common self-sabotaging behaviors to the neurotransmitter loops that underpin them. I'll explain it in detail so you can see why these behaviors happen and how your brain chemistry comes to play.

1. **Procrastination**

    Neurotransmitters involved: Dopamine + Cortisol
    - Dopamine: Drives motivation and reward-seeking. If the reward feels too far off or uncertain, your brain prioritizes immediate gratification instead. That's why scrolling social media or reorganizing your desk feels "better" than tackling a big task.
    - Cortisol: High stress levels make a task feel threatening. Your brain interprets it as risky, so avoidance feels safer.

    How it plays out: You delay an important task to avoid the stress of potential failure, which gives temporary relief. Dopamine rewards the short-term comfort, reinforcing the avoidance loop.

2. **Quitting or Walking Away Too Soon**

    Neurotransmitters involved: Dopamine + Cortisol + GABA
    - Dopamine: Lack of immediate reward from a job, project, or relationship can make the long-term benefits feel invisible.
    - Cortisol: Fear of conflict, criticism, or stress makes staying in the situation feel unsafe.
    - GABA: Low calming signals reduce your ability to tolerate discomfort, making you more likely to exit situations prematurely.

    How it plays out: Your brain interprets the challenge as "dangerous" and not worth the effort, so leaving provides immediate stress relief, but the long-term consequences reinforce the self-sabotage.

3. **Picking Fights or Reacting Impulsively**

   Neurotransmitters involved: Serotonin + Cortisol + GABA
   - Serotonin: Low levels reduce impulse control and patience, making you more irritable.
   - Cortisol: Heightened stress response perceives small conflicts as major threats.
   - GABA: Insufficient calming signals make emotional regulation harder.

   How it plays out: You argue over small things or respond defensively. It feels automatic, like a reflex. Short-term, it may release tension, but long-term, it damages relationships.

4. **Dating the "Wrong" People or Staying in Bad Relationships**

   Neurotransmitters involved: Oxytocin + Serotonin + Dopamine
   - Oxytocin: Heightens attachment and bonding, even to people who aren't a good match.
   - Serotonin: Low serotonin increases anxiety and can make you cling or feel unsafe when alone.
   - Dopamine: Chasing the highs of romance or novelty can override long-term compatibility considerations.

   How it plays out: Even if a relationship is unhealthy, your brain rewards the attachment and novelty, reinforcing repeated patterns. Emotional pain or conflict can even strengthen the loop in some cases (because your brain is wired to seek closure or resolution).

5. **Negative Self-Talk / Putting Yourself Down**

   Neurotransmitters involved: Serotonin + Cortisol
   - Serotonin: Low serotonin can make you focus on threats, including self-criticism.
   - Cortisol: Stress loops amplify the perceived consequences of failure.

How it plays out: Self-criticism triggers stress and low mood, reinforcing avoidance and inaction. Your brain treats the negative self-talk as "truth," which makes self-sabotage feel automatic.

6. **Avoiding Your Needs / Difficulty Saying No**

    Neurotransmitters involved: GABA + Serotonin + Cortisol

    - GABA: Low calming signals make confrontation feel overwhelming.
    - Serotonin: Low levels reduce assertiveness and confidence.
    - Cortisol: Stress response triggers fight-or-flight signals, so you choose "flight" (avoidance).

    How it plays out: You let others overstep or neglect your needs to avoid stress, conflict, or discomfort, reinforcing a pattern where your voice isn't heard.

Brain Inflammation and Mood Dysregulation

Sophie Papp, a 19-year-old from Victoria, British Columbia, was driving one afternoon in 2014 when her car flipped into a ravine. She survived, but the Sophie who opened her eyes after the coma wasn't the same person her family had known all her life. The accident had left her brain inflamed and shaken, and in the process it seemed to have rewritten her personality.

Before the crash, Sophie was quiet. She kept to herself, spoke only when spoken to, and slipped in and out of rooms almost unnoticed. After the coma, everything changed. She became talkative, restless, bursting with questions for anyone within reach. Nurses and doctors couldn't move through the ward without being stopped by her curiosity. One day she grilled a radiologist about brain anatomy, asking about the thalamus, the cerebellum, the fornix, terms she'd just picked up but was desperate to understand.

Her father brought her medical books from the library, and she devoured them late into the night, unable to stop. She was volatile. She laughed too hard, cried too suddenly, and felt overwhelmed by noises and lights most people could ignore. Everyday life became an overload. As she once described it, her senses had all been turned up too high, like the world itself was unbearable.

Her mother put it into words that still sting: "It was like losing a child, but a physical representation of that child is still living, and we had to get to know who she was." That's what brain inflammation and trauma can do. It doesn't just hurt the body. It can rearrange the person you are, in ways you never agreed to.

Sophie's story may sound extreme, but it shows something we don't always talk about: the brain is not just a box of thoughts and memories. It's tissue. It's an organ. Like every other organ in the body, it can become inflamed. When that happens, the ripple effects can reach far beyond headaches or fatigue. It can touch the very core of who you are, your moods, your energy, your stability.

Most of us don't connect mood swings or emotional storms with inflammation. We think of them as "just stress," or "just hormones," or "just who I am." In some cases, there's a deeper physical cause at play. Brain inflammation has been linked to anxiety, depression, irritability, sudden bursts of anger, and that flat emotional numbness people sometimes mistake for laziness.

When neurons are under siege from inflammation, the chemical signals they rely on, serotonin, dopamine, glutamate, don't flow the way they should. Circuits that normally keep emotions balanced start to misfire. The result is mood dysregulation that doesn't respond to pep talks or sheer willpower, because the problem isn't only psychological, it's biological.

So how do you know if what you're going through is "normal moodiness" or something that might be tied to inflammation? The truth is, there's no single red flag. It's about patterns and persistence. If your mood changes are sudden, severe, or feel completely out of step with what's happening in your life, it's worth paying attention. If you find yourself swinging from rage to tears without any clear trigger, or if your energy crashes alongside foggy thinking, headaches, or other physical symptoms, that might be your brain's way of saying, "something's off."

There are also medical conditions where brain inflammation is more likely, autoimmune diseases, long viral infections, concussions, and certain metabolic disorders. If you've gone through one of these and your moods haven't felt like your own since, that's not something to brush aside. It doesn't always mean something catastrophic is happening, but it does mean your brain might be working under stress.

Knowing when to see a doctor comes down to honesty with yourself. Ask: are these mood changes making it hard to function? Are they straining your relationships? Do they feel alien to who you know yourself to be? If the answer is yes, it's not a weakness to ask for help. It's wisdom.

A doctor would run tests, look at inflammation markers, or dig into other health issues that could be fueling the problem. Sometimes the path forward is treatment, sometimes it's lifestyle shifts, sometimes it's medication. What matters is that you're not left carrying it alone, thinking it's all in your head.

Hormonal Hiccups

My friend Cathy has the most amazing set of twins I have ever met. Jason and Janie are like night and day, yet somehow perfectly matched. Jason has always been blunt. From the time he could talk, he had no filter. If you asked him how your new dress looked, he'd say, "Weird."

If you asked about dinner, he'd announce to the whole table, "Too salty." Janie was the opposite, gentle, sweet, and endlessly considerate. She'd soften his words for him, pat your hand, and say, "It's still nice." Watching them together was like watching comedy in motion: Jason throwing stones, Janie running behind picking them up.

What cracked Cathy up even more was their growth. For years, Janie towered over Jason. At birthday parties, she looked like the older sibling, and Jason looked like the little brother tagging along. Cathy teased him about it, reminding him that patience pays off. She was right. A few years later, Jason shot up like bamboo, his voice cracked, his frame filled out, and suddenly he was towering over his sister. Janie never caught up.

Childhood growth is fairly steady for boys and girls, but when puberty comes, hormones take center stage. Estrogen pushes girls into their growth spurt earlier, which is why Janie shot up first.

Testosterone enters the scene later in boys but keeps working longer and harder, which is how Jason left her behind in the end. Hormones don't just sculpt height. They shape bones, muscles, fat distribution, even the wiring of the brain.

Girls' brains tend to mature earlier in certain areas, especially those linked to language and emotional regulation. Boys' brains mature a little later, but they develop differently in regions tied to spatial skills and problem solving. That's why Jason and Janie weren't just different in size; they thought and reacted differently too. Hormones were already sketching their personalities in ways they couldn't see.

Hormones might feel like abstract biology, but we bump into their influence all the time. Think of a teenager suddenly obsessed with how they look. That self-consciousness isn't just vanity, it's estrogen, progesterone, or testosterone changing how the brain interprets social feedback.

Or think of a new mother whose emotions swing wildly. The drop in estrogen and progesterone after birth can make even the strongest women feel fragile, anxious, or like strangers in their own skin.

Then there's stress. Cortisol, the stress hormone, is behind those sharp mood swings we often dismiss as "just having a bad day." Ever snapped at someone over something tiny, then felt silly afterward? That was cortisol talking, not your "true self." Sleep-deprived nights also mess with hormonal balance. Miss a few nights of good sleep, and ghrelin and leptin, the hormones that control hunger, get out of sync, making you crave junk food you normally wouldn't even think about.

Even small, everyday choices trigger hormonal ripples. Exercise boosts endorphins and dopamine, which can shift your whole outlook in under an hour. That's why a short walk sometimes feels like medicine. Coffee spikes adrenaline, giving that sharp buzz, but pushes it too far and it tips into jitters. These little hormonal pushes and pulls are constant reminders that our inner chemistry is always shaping our thoughts and feelings, often louder than logic.

People often say men are logical while women are emotional. It's an old stereotype, but like many stereotypes, it grew from kernels of truth mixed with cultural exaggeration. Hormones play a part here. Testosterone, the hormone most associated with men, influences risk-taking, competitiveness, and a kind of tunnel-vision focus. Estrogen and progesterone, more central in women, are tied to emotional regulation, empathy, and how the brain processes stress.

This doesn't mean men lack emotion or women lack logic. It means hormones shape the way each brain leans under pressure. A surge of testosterone might push a man to act decisively, sometimes recklessly, while a rise in estrogen can make a woman more attuned to subtle social cues. Cortisol complicates the picture further. Under high stress, women often release more cortisol than men, which can heighten emotional responses. Men, fueled by testosterone, may appear more "calm" or detached, even if they're not.

These differences start young. Girls often develop stronger emotional vocabulary earlier, while boys tend toward spatial problem solving. It's not destiny, social expectations and upbringing magnify the gap, but hormones laid some groundwork. By adulthood, those hormonal tendencies can make it look like women are more emotional and men are more logical, when really both are using different toolkits their hormones helped sharpen.

Confidence is another place hormones step into the spotlight. For men, testosterone brings that steady sense of "I've got this." It's not just about muscles or aggression; it's the quiet push that fuels motivation, energy, and even resilience. When testosterone dips, whether from age, stress, or medical conditions, men report feeling flat, tired, or less capable, even if nothing else in life has changed.

For women, estrogen does something similar. In balance, it makes many women feel socially open, energetic, even radiant. That's why during certain points in the menstrual cycle, confidence naturally rises. When estrogen or progesterone swing too far, too high, too low, the fallout can be brutal. Anxiety, mood swings, self-doubt, or even depressive spells steps in.

So what can we do? The truth is, we can't micromanage our hormones like we do our schedules, but we can support balance. Sleep is one of the biggest stabilizers. Without enough rest, cortisol spikes, testosterone drops, and appetite hormones go haywire.

Food matters too, steady meals, less processed sugar, enough protein and healthy fats all give the body what it needs to keep hormone levels steady.

Still, sometimes imbalance isn't something you can out-sleep or out-eat. If mood swings are extreme, if confidence crashes without reason, or if fatigue lingers despite rest, it may be worth checking out. Recognizing when it's your biology speaking, not your "true self," is the first step toward getting help. Hormones might be invisible, but they are powerful. Knowing when they've crossed from normal fluctuations into genuine disruption can save months, even years, of unnecessary suffering.

Why Emotional Experiences "Feel" More True Than Rational Ones

Have you ever noticed how emotions just hijack everything? Like, you *know* logically that you're overreacting, that your fear or shame or anger is blown out of proportion, but your body doesn't care. It's gripping you anyway. That's why we replay conversations, stew about stuff that's already done. It's not laziness. It's biology.

Your emotional brain doesn't weigh context. It doesn't care if it's rational. It cares about immediacy, survival, and relevance. And because of how memory works, emotional events stick like superglue. Stress hormones make them extra vivid in your brain. That's why you remember exactly how bad that argument felt last year, but you forget what you had for breakfast. Emotional experiences feel truer than rational ones. They *look* like reality, even when they're chemically amplified.

Then there's the loop. Spiraling thoughts are just the brain keeping the alarm bell ringing. The amygdala thinks something is unresolved or urgent. Logic tries to intervene, but it's slow, quiet. So the same fear, shame, or anger runs in circles. You tell yourself to calm down. Doesn't work. You're physically locked into the loop.

But there are cracks in the system. Detachment isn't suppression, it's noticing. Naming the emotion, even internally, "this is anger," "this is anxiety", turns on the thinking part of your brain a little. Noticing what's happening in your body, tight shoulders, racing heart, shallow breathing, reminds you this is a temporary state, not a statement of fact. Separate thought from fact. Micro-breaks help. Move, stretch, breathe, step outside. And for the love of everything, don't judge yourself. Curiosity works better than criticism.

The beauty in all this? Once you get it, you start noticing patterns. Spirals pop up and you see them coming. You pause instead of reacting. Over time, you literally train the thinking part of your brain to calm the alarm system. Emotions don't vanish. You still feel fear, shame, excitement, rage. However, they stop dictating what your reality *is*. You get to experience them, not get trapped by them.

Chapter Summary

- At the most basic level, a thought begins as an electrical impulse. Your brain contains about 86 billion neurons. Each neuron can connect to thousands of others, creating trillions of possible connections. These connections form circuits and networks, kind of like overlapping highways of information.
- Self-sabotage is when you end up working against yourself, even though you want something different. It's when your actions, or sometimes your lack of action, block the very goals you care about.
- Is self-sabotage your fault? The short answer is no, self-sabotage is not simply your fault. Most of the time, the behaviors you call sabotage started as survival strategies.

6

The Placebo Effect of Belief

> If Placebo were a drug, they would no doubt be pure heroin - dangerous, mysterious and totally addictive.
> —Brian Molko

The very first time a placebo was used in anything close to a scientific sense goes back further than most people think. Doctors have always known that sometimes people feel better just because they believe they're being treated. Ancient physicians, like those in Greece, China, or medieval Europe, would give patients remedies that didn't really have active ingredients, but they didn't call them "placebos." They just thought healing often needed ritual, reassurance, or faith.

The word placebo itself comes from Latin, meaning "I shall please." It was first used in medicine in the late 18th century. Around 1785, the word appears in the New Medical Dictionary to describe a medicine that had no real therapeutic effect, given mostly to comfort the patient. In practice, doctors would sometimes prescribe sugar pills, bread pills, or harmless tonics when they thought the illness was untreatable, or when they suspected the patient's symptoms were more emotional than physical. It was a way of doing something rather than nothing.

The first time the placebo was formally tested in a modern trial happened in the 18th century as well. One of the earliest famous examples was in 1799, when an English physician named John Haygarth tested the supposed healing power of "Perkins tractors."

These were metal rods that a quack doctor claimed could draw disease out of the body. Haygarth suspected they were fake, so he tried an experiment: he treated patients with both the real metal rods and identical-looking wooden rods. The patients improved just as much with the wooden ones as with the metal ones. That's one of the first clear demonstrations of the placebo effect in action.

From there, the idea developed slowly. In the 20th century, especially after World War II, placebos became central in medical research. Doctors realised they needed to compare real drugs against something neutral, so they started using placebo-controlled trials. By the 1950s, the "randomised, double-blind, placebo-controlled trial" had become the gold standard for testing new medicines.

What makes that old story about wooden rods so striking isn't just that people got better from nothing, it's that their bodies responded as if the lie was real. Muscles relaxed, pain eased, symptoms shifted. The brain didn't need to wait around for some proof; it created its own.

That single moment in history opened a door into something much bigger: the way belief itself can change biology. Once you see that, you can't really unsee it.

Belief as a Biological Force

There's this study I always think about. Steele and Aronson back in the 90s had Black college students sit for a test. When they told them it was an "intelligence" test, their scores dropped. Same students, same test, but when they said it was just problem-solving, the scores went back up.

Nothing in their actual ability had changed in that moment, only the belief in what the test meant. That belief was enough to weigh down their performance. Their brains were fighting stereotypes, stress, self-doubt.

That's what convinces me that belief isn't just an abstract thing. It can be a biological force. It doesn't stay politely in your head.

You see it in the placebo effect all the time. People swallow sugar pills, convinced it's medicine, and their pain lessens, inflammation eases, sometimes even their symptoms shrink. This is not fake at all. Their bodies are releasing endorphins and shifting cortisol levels because of a story their mind decided to believe.

The opposite happens too. That's the nocebo effect. A harmless pill can give you real nausea if you believe it will. Because the brain and the body are wired together so tightly, belief can tilt you toward healing or toward decline. That's why it matters what you believe about yourself when no one else is listening.

So how exactly does belief become biology? It's through the stress pathways, the reward system, and the immune network. The brain doesn't wait for evidence before it reacts. If you believe something, your body moves as if it's already true.

Take stress. If you believe you're in danger, even if you're not, your body floods with cortisol and adrenaline. Heart rate rises, blood vessels tighten, digestion slows. Over time, if you carry a steady belief like "I'm never safe" or "I'll fail no matter what," your body lives in that stress chemistry. It's like holding down the gas pedal on your car without ever letting up, you wear the engine out.

The immune system listens too. Optimistic beliefs tend to strengthen immune responses, while pessimistic ones weaken them. Think about that for a second, your white blood cells, the things fighting infection, actually perform differently depending on what you believe about your chances.

Beliefs also steer habits, and habits reinforce biology. If you believe a morning walk helps, you'll take it, and that act boosts mood and lowers inflammation. If you believe nothing helps, you'll skip it, and biology drifts into decline. The brain writes scripts, and the body plays them out.

Wrong beliefs can slip in quietly and do just as much damage. Sometimes they come from family, sometimes from culture, sometimes from old experiences that never got challenged. Because beliefs affect feelings and biology, they can feel true even when they're not.

The way to avoid those wrong beliefs starts with paying attention to how your body reacts. If your stomach knots every time you make a small mistake, maybe the belief underneath is "mistakes mean I'm a failure." That belief is going to keep stress hormones high every time life doesn't go smoothly.

Another place to watch is culture. Society hands out wrong beliefs all the time. "Men don't cry." "Rest is laziness." "If you're not constantly busy, you're worthless." These aren't facts, they're stories.

There are also self-fulfilling beliefs. If you think "I always get sick in the cold," your body's stress response primes you for it, and you're more vulnerable. If you believe "I'll never lose weight," your motivation shuts down, and biology simply follows the script of inactivity.

Some examples sting because they're so common:

- "I'm not good enough." That one keeps the body in constant stress mode.
- "It runs in my family, so I'll get it too." That belief can kill motivation for prevention, even though lifestyle changes often matter just as much as genes.
- "Rest is weakness." That one leads straight to burnout, stripping away recovery your body desperately needs.

So what do you do with these wrong beliefs once you notice them? Rejecting them outright isn't enough. The mind hates a blank space. *You have to replace them with beliefs that are both true and believable.* Not something fake or grandiose, but something that your body can lean on. Instead of "I'm not good enough," you hold on to "I'm still learning, but I've handled hard things before." That belief signals safety to your nervous system. Instead of "rest is laziness," shift to "rest is recovery, and recovery makes me stronger." The body calms when it hears that, and stress chemistry eases.

It also helps to look at your environment. Beliefs are contagious. If you spend time with people who believe aging is nothing but decline, your biology will echo that. If you're around those who believe aging can bring wisdom and resilience, your biology benefits from that script instead.

It's worth checking in from time to time. What you believed at 15 might not serve you at 35. Some beliefs that once protected you, like "I can't trust anyone" after being hurt, start to poison you if they stick around too long. Ask yourself: is this belief keeping my body safe, or keeping it stuck?

Expectancy Loops

They call it the *law of first mention* in some circles. The idea is simple: the first way you're introduced to something has a way of sticking, sometimes for life. Your brain takes that first definition, that first taste, and stamps it down like a label. Even if reality later proves it wrong, that first impression stays for a very long time.

Like the first time I ever tasted olives. I was about seven, and I stole one from the top of a pizza. I thought it was candy because it looked glossy, round, almost like a grape. Then, bam, salt and bitterness exploded in my mouth. My seven-year-old brain wrote down a note: *olives are disgusting and should never be trusted.* It took me until I was in my twenties to even try them again, and even then, the old disgusting memory hovered like a warning.

Same with certain songs. If your first mention of a song was during a breakup, that song carries heartbreak forever, even if it's objectively catchy. Or maybe the first time you tried driving, someone yelled at you for stalling, and now, even years later, you grip the wheel with that echo in your body.

The brain loves shortcuts, and "first mention" is one of its favorites. It saves energy. Why reevaluate olives every time you see them? The brain says, *we've been here before, and it was bad, let's not waste time. Been there, done that.* First mention becomes the default setting. Which is efficient, sure, but not always accurate. Sometimes the brain keeps running an old program long after it's outdated.

It's surprisingly easy for our minds to clutch the painful stuff tighter than the good. You could have ten happy childhood memories, but the one where someone mocked you will stick louder, brighter, sharper.

Trauma takes that rule and amplifies it. When something painful or scary happens, the brain tags it as "priority memory." The nervous system wires itself to be on alert, scanning for anything that resembles that past hurt. A slammed door can sound like the start of a fight. A smell can yank you back years. Even if the present moment is safe, the brain projects the past onto it.

What makes it harder is how embodied it feels. I need you to know that trauma isn't just a thought, it's a body memory. That brings us to how past experiences rewire future outcomes. The brain doesn't sit around waiting for life to happen. It constantly guesses what's coming next based on what's happened before.

Think about walking into a dark room. Your brain predicts where the couch is, where the table sits, how many steps until the doorframe. You don't consciously measure it every time, you rely on memory, expectation, prediction. Most of the time, that's incredibly useful. Until the furniture gets moved, and suddenly your shin takes the hit.

That's how life works on a bigger scale too. If your past experiences tell your brain that love equals abandonment, it predicts that future love will hurt. So you tend to sabotage relationships without fully knowing why. If your past taught you that failure equals humiliation, your brain predicts that trying again will bring shame, so it keeps you frozen.

Nocebo Thinking

Most people have heard of the placebo effect, where someone feels better simply because they believe a treatment will work, even if the "treatment" is just a bread pill. There's a darker twin to this phenomenon, and it's called the nocebo effect. Instead of belief creating healing, belief creates harm.

The word *nocebo* comes from Latin, meaning *"I shall harm"* (where placebo means *"I shall please"*). In practice, it describes situations where negative expectations or beliefs about a treatment or condition actually lead to worse symptoms.

For example, if a doctor warns a patient that a medication may cause headaches, the patient is far more likely to develop headaches, even if they're given a pill that contains no active drug at all. In clinical studies, nocebo effects are strikingly common. In fact, some trials report that more than half of patients taking a placebo still experience the side effects listed on the label, simply because they expected them.

Medical science has studied this extensively, because researchers need to separate genuine drug effects from expectation-driven effects. A famous case happened during chemotherapy trials: some patients who were given placebo pills reported losing their hair, vomiting, or feeling extreme fatigue, not because of the drug (they hadn't taken it yet), but because they believed that chemotherapy *always* caused those symptoms.

So has nocebo been "effective" in medical science? The short answer is: yes, but not in a positive way. It doesn't heal; it harms. Its "effectiveness" shows up in the reliability of its influence. Just as placebo can consistently boost recovery, nocebo can consistently make symptoms worse.

Nocebo thinking is when the same principle of the nocebo effect moves from the doctor's office into everyday life. It's the habit of expecting the worst and, in turn, training the body and brain to respond as if the worst is already happening.

For instance, if someone believes every stomach ache must be a sign of cancer, their stress response amplifies the pain. If someone believes they'll never sleep well, their anxiety around bedtime often ensures they don't. Nocebo thinking turns fear and expectation into a self-fulfilling loop.

It doesn't mean the symptoms are fake. The body really does change under the weight of negative expectation. Heart rate increases, cortisol spikes, muscles tighten, pain signals become sharper. In some cases, long-term nocebo thinking can worsen chronic conditions like migraines, irritable bowel syndrome, or fatigue.

Essentially, nocebo thinking is the mental habit of letting fear dictate how the body responds, often without realizing it.

Mostly, nocebo is harmful. It can heighten pain, worsen symptoms, make medications feel less effective, and create new health problems fueled by stress and expectation. In medicine, it's one of the biggest barriers to treatment adherence. Some patients stop life-saving drugs because they "feel" side effects that are actually nocebo-driven.

That said, there's one "beneficial" angle: the existence of the nocebo effect teaches us how powerful belief really is. By studying it, doctors and psychologists learn how to better frame conversations, how to reduce unnecessary fear, and how to support patients in ways that don't trigger harm. For patients, awareness of nocebo can create a pause, a chance to notice when fear itself might be driving some of their symptoms.

Self-Fulfilling Neural Pathways

Self-fulfilling prophecies are very real. It's the idea that what you expect can nudge you into actions that make the expectation come true. If you walk into a room already convinced no one will like you, chances are you'll avoid eye contact, give short answers, and carry an energy that pushes people away. Then you leave saying, "See? Nobody liked me."

It's not that your belief magically bent reality. It's that your belief shaped your behavior, and your behavior shaped the outcome. Teachers see this with students. If they believe one child is gifted, they'll unknowingly encourage them more, creating the very result they expected. The same goes the other way when low expectations choke potential.

We do this to ourselves too. Tell yourself often enough that you're not good at something, and you'll avoid chances to practice. No practice means no growth, which only proves your point. The prophecy fulfills itself.

Every time you think a thought, tiny signals race down a network of neurons. The more often you repeat that thought, the stronger the pathway becomes, like walking a trail until it turns into a deep groove.

Over time, this pattern becomes automatic. You don't even realize you're reinforcing it. The brain, trying to be efficient, keeps sending you down the same mental highway, even when it hurts you. That's the essence of a self-fulfilling neural pathway: a thought, a reaction, an outcome that proves the thought true, and then the brain wiring itself to expect the same again.

The hopeful part is this: pathways aren't fixed. The brain can unlearn. It takes effort and awareness, but new grooves can be made, and old ones can weaken.

If you usually avoid situations where you fear failure, push yourself to try small, low-stakes versions. Each successful experience gives your brain evidence that the old pathway isn't the only option.

Cognitive Dissonance: How the Brain Edits Reality to Match Belief

If you stare at blue light through yellow lenses, you won't see blue or yellow, you'll see green. Your eyes don't report two separate colors to your brain. They mix. Your brain edits what it thinks you're seeing so that the world feels neat, predictable, consistent. That's what the brain does all the time. It edits. It smooths over contradictions so you can walk around without constantly tripping on things that don't add up.

That's basically what cognitive dissonance is. It's the brain's built-in discomfort when what you do and what you believe don't line up. Or when you learn something that clashes with what you already know. Sometimes it changes your behavior, sometimes your belief, and a lot of the time it just makes up a tidy excuse.

In the 1950s, Psychologists Festinger and Carlsmith had students do this mind-numbingly boring task, turning little knobs for an hour. Then they asked some of the students to tell the next participant that it was actually fun. Some were paid $20 for lying, others just $1.

Afterward, the ones who were paid $20 admitted it was boring. Easy, lying for that much money made sense. The ones who only got $1? They convinced themselves it really was fun. Their brains couldn't stand the idea of lying for so little. So instead of admitting "I lied for almost nothing," they rewrote the memory: "Maybe it was kind of interesting after all." That's dissonance at work, the brain stitching over a tear in the fabric.

A smoker knows cigarettes are bad but says, "My uncle smoked till 90." A friend stays in a toxic relationship and says, "They're not always that bad." You buy an overpriced gadget and later say, "It's an investment." Your brain hates holding two clashing truths, so it edits.

This editing doesn't just happen with little things. It shapes entire identities. If you believe you're a good person but you hurt someone, dissonance kicks in. To resolve it, you either admit, "Maybe I wasn't good at that moment," or more commonly, you explain it away: "They provoked me." The brain prefers protecting your self-image over tearing it down.

Dissonance can be healthy or unhealthy. Sometimes it nudges you toward growth. Say you value honesty but you lied, that sting of discomfort would push you to align your actions better. Other times it traps you in rationalization. You don't want to change your behavior, so you bend your belief instead. It's easier to say, "Exercise is overrated" than to actually start working out.

This is why marketing, politics, even religion lean on dissonance. Advertisers tell you, "If you're a good parent, you'll buy this." If you don't buy it, your brain feels that static, you either change your view ("I guess I don't need it") or you give in and buy, just to silence the noise. Politicians use it too, when new evidence contradicts your loyalty, it's easier to attack the evidence than admit you were wrong.

What makes this both fascinating and frightening is that your brain is constantly editing reality. The edits don't feel like edits, they feel like truth. Like looking through yellow lenses: you don't think, "This is blue plus yellow." You just see green.

So when you find yourself justifying things, or holding on to a belief that feels oddly untouchable, it might not be the pure truth you're clinging to, it might be your brain protecting you from dissonance. Sometimes that's harmless. Sometimes it keeps you stuck.

The question isn't whether dissonance happens, it always does. The question is whether you'll let those edits keep you in a loop, or whether you'll use that uncomfortable static as a signal that something in your life needs to shift.

The Biology of Hope vs. Fear

My friend Andaline once told me about the longest week of her life. She had found a lump on her breast and was waiting for the test results. Every morning she'd wake up very worried and fearful. Fear painted everything black.

She'd snapped at her husband for no reason, couldn't eat properly, and found herself reading medical forums at 2 a.m., convincing herself it was cancer. Then, strangely, there were moments when the storm inside her cleared. She'd think, maybe it's nothing… Maybe I'll be fine.

In those moments she could breathe again, even laugh at something on TV, only to feel guilty after, as if laughter was too light for the weight she was carrying. That week was a tug-of-war between fear and hope, and her body carried every pull of the rope.

Hope and fear are two sides of the same coin. Both are ways of imagining the future, only tilted in opposite directions. Fear leans toward danger and worst-case scenarios, hope tilts toward possibility and survival. Fear contracts the world; it makes us cautious, keeps us scanning for threats. Hope expands the world; it lets us risk, try, and keep walking even when logic whispers to stop.

Both emotions feel very real, even though neither is proof of what will happen. That's the trick: hope and fear are rehearsals. They're mental dress rehearsals for futures we haven't lived yet. Which brings us to the heart of it: hope and fear aren't just feelings, they're full-body experiences.

The problem is that modern fears don't end the way ancient ones did. In the past, you either escaped the lion or you didn't. Either way, the surge of stress would end. Today, fear lingers. You worry about money for weeks, rehearse breakups in your head, wait for medical results like Andaline did. The stress hormones keep flowing, and your body pays the price. Chronic fear wears down the immune system, strains the heart, and leaves you restless, fatigued, even sick. It's not "just in your head." It's in your bloodstream, your muscles, your sleep.

Hope works differently. Instead of cortisol and adrenaline flooding your system, hope leans on chemicals like dopamine and oxytocin. Dopamine is the brain's way of saying, something good might happen, keep going. Oxytocin softens you toward connection, toward trust. Together, they create a state where the body feels safe enough to heal, safe enough to take chances, safe enough to rest.

Researchers have seen this play out in hospitals. Patients who feel hopeful about recovery tend to heal faster, need fewer painkillers, and show stronger immune responses after surgery. Hope doesn't guarantee survival, but it changes the biology of the fight. It keeps the body from drowning in stress.

On smaller scales, you can feel it too. When you have a hopeful outlook, you breathe a little easier. Your shoulders drop. You find yourself open to laughing, to reaching out to a friend, to trying again tomorrow. Hope literally widens your field of vision. Fear keeps your eyes darting for danger; hope lets you notice the sunrise.

Most of life is lived somewhere between those two forces. Too much fear, and you shrink into survival mode, unable to move forward. Too much blind hope, and you risk ignoring real dangers. The balance is not silencing fear or forcing optimism. You have to notice which one is holding the rope in your hands, and remembering that both are rehearsals, not facts.

Chapter Summary

- Belief isn't just an abstract thing. It can be a biological force. It doesn't stay politely in your head.
- When something painful or scary happens, the brain tags it as "priority memory." The nervous system wires itself to be on alert, scanning for anything that resembles that past hurt.
- Nocebo is harmful. It can heighten pain, worsen symptoms, make medications feel less effective, and create new health problems fueled by stress and expectation.
- Self-fulfilling prophecies are very real. It's the idea that what you expect can nudge you into actions that make the expectation come true
- Dissonance can be healthy or unhealthy. Sometimes it nudges you toward growth. Say you value honesty but you lied, that sting of discomfort would push you to align your actions better. Other times it traps you in rationalization. You don't want to change your behavior, so you bend your belief instead. It's easier to say, "Exercise is overrated" than to actually start working out.

7

How Your Memories Lie

> What happened in the past that was painful has a great deal to do with what we are today, but revisiting this painful past can contribute little or nothing to what we need to do now.
> —William Glasser

Memories are powerful data in our brain, and their presence can influence what we believe, how we behave, and what we think about ourselves and others around us.

Here's an example of how this happens. Mia once responded to a question about some illusory childhood experience. She said that she was just a child when her mother told her that a creature lived beneath the toilet bowl.

According to her mother, the creature lived on a tiny island just after the U-bend. It drew its breath through the same pipe that the toilet flushed. Therefore, if Mia stayed too long on the toilet seat, the creature would suffocate and react furiously.

Mia recounted that she was terrified by the idea of harming a hidden, helpless being or being hurt herself. So, she developed a habit of rushing every bathroom visit. After many years, she forgot the story, but the habit stayed. As an adult, she never quite understood why she could hardly relax in the toilet. It was after a casual chat with her mom that she realised that the whole tale had been made up. It was just her mother's strategy to hasten her dawdling child.

But here's the thing: Mia had it good. Many kids were not so "lucky." Many had to cope with abuse of all kinds under the guise of parenting. As a result, many people grew up with distorted views about life and themselves.

These views are powered by memories, and what those memories mean to the sufferer. For instance, a kid who suffered emotional abuse may grow up with an insecure attachment style, leading to problems with forming meaningful relationships. These issues will not magically resolve themselves just because the kid who is now a man has met a great woman. Chances are, no matter how sweet that relationship gets, he will ruin it. Not because he is a bad person, but because he is a man who is still hurting and hasn't healed.

This is how hanging on to those memories and living by them as your reality will interrupt your life and keep you rehashing your trauma again and again to devastating effect.

In this chapter, we'll zoom in more on some memories we sometimes hold on to as our reality, which can diminish the quality and fullness of our lives. This will help you reevaluate some of your beliefs and behavior, their origins, and check if they are even true.

The False Memory Factory

In 2010, Meredith Maran published *My Lie: A Story of False Memory*, a book born from an experience that gripped America in the 1980s and 90s. It all began with the infamous McMartin preschool trial, when parents of children came forward with disturbing claims of sexual abuse. These allegations were never proven in court, but they set off a nationwide wave of false memories, false accusations, and fractured lives before the case collapsed.

At 37, Maran herself falsely accused her father of sexual abuse. It took her about 10 years to realize that he was innocent. However, it was too late. In an interview with the American Psychological Association (APA), Elizabeth Loftus, a professor at the University of California, Irvine, talked about how human memories can evolve as new information, ideas, thoughts, and suggestive ideas, including misinformation, enter into our conscious awareness (Luna, 2019). These 'new' entries can contaminate or alter existing memories.

Through different engagements, like therapy, group talks, etc., people can be led to believe that they've had some brutal experience in the past, which could be from a non-existent event from the recent past or from their childhood. The result is that these false memories would influence people's thoughts, behaviors, and intentions, as it did in the McMartin trial.

Loftus explained that those who were victims of that sex-abuse panic were made to bring up some repressed memories when they visited a therapist due to a mental health condition like depression and anxiety. It was during those sessions that patients were led to remember some brutal experiences in the past, which they supposedly repressed until the therapy session brought them back. In response, the patients went ahead to prosecute people they thought had victimized them based on a false memory.

Following the eventual realization of the innocence of the people they had accused, does it mean that people can completely repress memories of unpleasant experiences, become completely unaware of them, then later bring them back? A related question to this is whether the brain completely forgets memories.

Whether memories can be repressed or not has been a subject of fierce debate between memory researchers and clinicians. This doesn't mean repressed memories don't exist; however, the danger of these memories is that they can be influenced or even created by suggestions during therapy (Hanson-Baiden, 2022).

In countering clinicians, some memory researchers revealed that when people are asked to recall events that never happened, especially alongside real ones, they tend to believe those false events as true. This led them to suggest that false memories can be perceived as real, just like actual experiences. Therefore, the patient in the therapy session will find it difficult to differentiate between what really happened and what was imagined.

According to Loftus, memories work like a Wikipedia page, so you can edit whatever you feel the need to. However, just as you can edit it, so can other people (Seligson, 2015). False memory occurs when a vulnerable person, especially someone who is highly suggestible, is led by a trusted authority figure to believe and remember an event that never actually happened.

During her interview with APA, Loftus also established that the mind's technology is quite a delicate one, as false memories can be planted in people's minds with differing intentions. Some are good, while others are not, but the mind accepts them all. Since you now know that your mind can be manipulated, you might need to ask if your memories can be trusted. This question isn't to shame you or cause confusion, especially if you've used the services of a therapist extensively. It's to ensure that what you've held as truth is checked to ensure that it is actually true and not a false memory.

It also doesn't imply that everything you recall having happened at some points in your life is false. I just want you to be aware that what we refer to as our memories is more complex than we can fully comprehend (BetterHelp Editorial Team, 2025).

You may want to revisit memories that make you think less of yourself. Don't you think so, too? If you've believed a memory for so long, and all it does to you is to develop self-sabotaging behavioral patterns, it should be questioned. What truth lies behind that memory? Even if you've convinced yourself time and again that the memory is true, it's beneficial to you to still question it.

Do you know why? Well, I'd say, why not? Why should your life be on a downward slope or troubled every time because of something that allegedly happened in the past? You deserve a healthier life. You should be doing more than you've been doing, but those memories are standing in the way, and they're messing with your mental well-being. That's the reason why they need to be checked.

Trauma as a Loop, Not a Moment

Can you imagine being stuck in one month, even though you've gone on to live out more of that month in other years? Actually, a traumatic event can make this happen, like it did to Avery.

Before she turned 18, an experience redefined how she saw the month of July. It was so vivid that her body remembered before her mind could. Almost a decade later, the month of July still gave her shivers as she relived the experience again and again.

Avery was only fifteen then, excited to visit a boy she had liked for a while. She dressed up, feeling hopeful, expectant. But what began as an innocent visit quickly turned into something she couldn't stop. Her voice said no, her hands resisted, but her strength waned with each attempt as he forced himself on her. She remembered how she walked back home in silence, with a painful memory she couldn't heal or share.

Shame wouldn't let her speak, so she kept quiet. Fear was her worst tormentor during that period. Time wore on at the event; she tried to forget and move on, but the memory stayed. Sometimes it screamed, at other times it stayed buried, but it was always present. For years, she didn't understand why she recoiled at touch, why she avoided relationships, why a certain month or places triggered anxiety she couldn't explain.

Avery, like many folks who have been traumatized, hasn't truly left that one moment when they experienced a traumatic event. They're still stuck there even after they've tried to move on in life. Moving on is a good thing, but the problem with it comes when they try to convince themselves that they've put all that behind them; the baggage from that trauma goes with them everywhere until they're able to begin to heal from it.

Moving on without healing will result in a constant replay of that event whenever something in the present moment triggers that experience. In response, they'll react with unpleasant emotions without really understanding why they reacted the way they did. They'll struggle with negative thoughts and self-sabotaging habits.

The reason this happens is that the brain hasn't been able to fully comprehend that traumatic event. So, instead of storing it like a past event, the brain treats it like an ongoing event, or something that could still happen. That's more like experiencing a song over and over again by putting it on a loop. The difference is that the effects from a trauma loop cause fear, shame, and guilt over and over again, but a music loop soothes.

(Bradfield 2022) explained that the trauma loop is really just the brain getting used to a certain pattern. When someone goes through repeated traumatic experiences, the brain forms a kind of shortcut in the nervous system to respond to those situations. Therefore, each time it happens, stress chemicals flood the brain, and over time, the brain gets used to functioning in that intense, stressed-out state.

Unfortunately, all that stress gets stuck. The thinking part of the brain struggles to make sense of what happened, so the trauma doesn't really get processed. For many survivors, that means they lose the ability to find meaning. Instead, the brain creates a well-worn path that keeps bringing them back to that same emotional place.

The more this path is used, the stronger it becomes. It's like making a trail in the woods. The first time is rough, but the more you walk it, the clearer and easier it gets. The brain does the same; it often chooses what's familiar, even if it's unhealthy.

So if your default response to stress becomes rage or shutting down, it's not because you want to react that way. It's because that path in the brain has become the easiest to take. (Rapkoch 2024) also explained that a trauma loop is one of the ways the body attempts to defend itself against likely threats. The way our bodies react to traumatic events is different for everyone. That's why trauma should be understood through each person's own experience, even if two or more people had similar experiences. Two people can experience the same thing, but only one might be traumatized. So, yes, your experience is unique. Still, you're not alone. Numerous survivors of trauma experience these loops you're experiencing. To heal from this, new neural paths need to be created, and the associated acts need to be practiced till they become stronger than the old ones.

If you're trying to figure out whether what you're going through is a trauma loop, especially when certain memories, places, or people set off your trauma response, here are some signs to notice:

- Disorientation
- Intrusive thoughts of the event
- Avoiding specific triggers linked to the event
- Nightmares
- Disrupted sleeping and eating habits
- Social isolation
- Extreme alertness
- Irritability
- Panic and anxiety attacks
- Depression
- Detachment from others
- Fear
- Shame
- Shock
- Guilt

This isn't an exhaustive list, but if two, three, or more of these are familiar, then chances are high that you're in a trauma loop.

Emotional Tagging

It's a common habit of the human brain to store events and experiences by how they made us feel. This store of emotions greatly influences how we feel when we want to make decisions, and if we go through with them at all. Finkelstein et al. (2019) in their management book, titled *Think Again: Why Good Leaders Make Bad Decisions and How to Keep It From Happening to You*, stated as much, describing emotional tagging as one of the brain's core mechanisms, whereby past events are stored along with emotional tags that influence future decision making.

There's a part of your brain called the amygdala, the part responsible for processing emotions, especially those you can link to survival, like fear and pleasure (Carter, 2024). Then, there's another part known as the hippocampus, which is in charge of handling how you form memories and store them.

Whenever you experience an emotionally charged event, the amygdala gets highly active. In that state, it alerts the hippocampus, which in turn marks the experience with an emotional tag. According to Carter (2024), when an event is tagged, it stands out and is easier for the brain to recall because they're crucial for survival and making critical decisions. A common example is a kid tagging fire with pain because they got burned one time. This would make the kid avoid fire as much as possible. Another example is a lady who tags swimming with peace or joy because that's the activity that relaxes her the most.

Some studies show that memories having emotional tags are usually vivid and tend to shape our future choices. Also, in the context of their discussion, Finkelstein et al. established that emotional tagging can help assess situations and determine the right action plan. However, the other side to emotional tagging is that it can also be disastrous.

This happens because emotional tags are like cues that draw the brain's attention, keeping those memories easily accessible when needed. When the brain tags a traumatic event with fear or danger, the amygdala can react with fight-or-flight responses if the event is happening again, or when something similar is occurring in the present.

This reaction triggers a cycle of actions. First, a signal is sent to the hypothalamus and adrenal glands, and then they'll release stress hormones. What you'll likely notice next is an increase in your heart rate, your breathing speeds up, and your muscles tense. All this happens because the present event triggered a memory tagged as a threat. This will still happen even if the present event is harmless.

In most cases, you may not understand why you react the way you do when you recall a past event. Emotional tagging is a possible explanation for your actions. Don't beat yourself up for this; it's your brain that doesn't know how to distinguish between a real-time threat and a strongly tagged fearful memory.

Though emotional tagging can be a great tool for making positive decisions, in the context of traumatic experiences, it would cause more harm than good. Let's take a product developer as an example. During one of his presentations, he faced a lot of harsh criticism for one failed project. Oblivious to his brain's activities, fear of rejection became his reaction to presentations. Worst of all, he became afraid of presenting bold ideas. He'd rather opt for something he considers safe instead of sticking his head out for groundbreaking innovations.

At times, what we consider 'safe' is actually the fear of stepping out. Hence, even when we have an opportunity to explore and dare to do bold things, our brain places an embargo on our participation because it's trying to 'protect us' from experiencing the same emotional hurt as we did in the past. However, even when our brain is trying to protect us from reliving the past, we're still living it because it still interferes with our daily lives in critical moments of decision-making.

One of the objectives of this chapter is to make you consciously aware of the reasons behind your thoughts and behavioral patterns. This awareness will also help you understand your past actions and decision-making, and you'll be able to make informed choices based on what you've learned. You'll understand why certain sights, sounds, or smells can cause sudden fear, tension, or even panic.

Going forward, instead of being reactive and driven by emotions in making crucial decisions, you'll be able to apply techniques that will help you pause and carefully decide on your next course of action. Also, understanding this connection will help you to recognise when your reactions are rooted in memory rather than in reality, giving you the chance to respond more wisely instead of purely out of instinct.

The Memory Editing Toolkit

As much as it seems like our brains are fixed on certain experiences, it's not as rigid as you think. The brain was designed to be malleable, to be able to change. That's why it's possible to learn some truth some years ago and learn an updated version later because the initial one is now obsolete. Yet, the brain doesn't get clogged up; rather, it adjusts and creates new neural pathways to embrace the new truth. Ultimately, this malleability also changes the entire experiences of a person.

This implies that your memories aren't cast in stone. They might look fixed, and the emotional responses that are tagged with them might look permanent, too. But not so. With this dynamic nature of the brain, the emotional responses can be "edited" to change your current experiences whenever those memories are triggered.

For instance, if every time you remember a traumatic car accident that happened some 5 years ago, you recoil and feel overwhelmed with sadness, it means you don't have to live with that reaction for the rest of your life. With the dynamic nature of the brain, your emotional response to the same memory can be edited. So, instead of feeling sad, you begin to feel a more positive emotion that doesn't affect your mental well-being or your efficiency that day.

In essence, your current emotional responses to that memory aren't final. You can rewire your brain to react better. The process involved in reshaping emotional responses to memories is what's known as memory reconsolidation.

(Osorio-Gómez et al. 2023) explained the dynamics of living things in reference to environmental changes. They shared that it's common for living things to remember things that help them survive. For instance, they remember where to get food, how to identify their mate, or how to avoid danger. Just like we've discussed earlier, sometimes, the emotional responses to traumatic memories could be a survival instinct triggered in a part of the brain to either fight or flee.

But Osorio-Gómez et al. shared that because of the dynamic nature of the world we live in, we can't rely on old information to cope. There will always be a need for us to adjust and adapt. One of the things that happens when people are stuck with memories so much that it influences their present experiences is that they don't grow. They're simply stuck.

Do you remember the illustration I gave at the beginning of this chapter, of remaining in a particular month despite experiencing many more of them in later years? That's what happens to a lot of people.

The sad thing is that they get left behind. Being left behind here means that some other folks who had similar experiences now have a whole different experience, other than the pain and hurt from the negative event. Now, they live happier and healthier.

However, if you're still stuck with the memory of the event with the tagged emotions, it's not your fault you're left behind. However, taking responsibility for what happens to you in the "now" is up to you. Do you know why? A lot of changes have happened around you, and time has worn on the event. It was a valid experience then. The emotions are valid too. But you now have a whole new environment that comprises new relationships, new opportunities, and new work or academic status. Allowing that memory to influence your current experience means that you've not adjusted to your new reality.

The good thing, however, is that Osorio-Gómez et al. affirmed that you can adjust your emotional responses. We've talked about how the memory can be manipulated; that's something that can be used to your advantage for better living experiences. That flexibility is leverage. Your brain can update and reshape any stored information. Leveraging this is the best way you can survive and live well within your current environment.

Professor Alain Brunet, a leading specialist dedicated to the study of PTSD, explained how PTSD patients can re-experience traumatic memories with serious intensity. He affirmed that it's usually accompanied by physical and emotional responses when they're triggered. In that moment, it would be like the patient is experiencing the trauma all over again.

Although there have been tools to question and reframe those experiences, one of which is CBT (Brunet 2025) stated that half of the patients often experience a relapse. That was what led to growing research on reconsolidation therapy. According to Brunet, reconsolidation therapy helps edit people's emotional response tagged with certain memories of traumatic events.

This therapeutic toolkit works like waiting for an open window to act. Brunet explained that anytime a memory is recalled, it becomes adjustable for a brief moment. That's the open window and the clue to update it before it stores again. The update process is what's known as memory reconsolidation. The goal of this therapeutic tool isn't to wipe out the memory; rather, it's to reduce its emotional sting.

During the procedure, patients are administered a small dose of propranolol, a common beta-blocker often prescribed to regulate high blood pressure and anxiety. When a PTSD patient is administered the drug, it doesn't wipe away their memory; instead, it minimizes their emotional distress attached to the memory. It disrupts the brain's usual process of reconsolidating those emotions.

Also, during the process, patients are directed to write a detailed account of their traumatic experience by focusing on the most distressing moments. So, after they've taken the propranolol, they will be asked to read the same account aloud in each session. As they go over this exercise, it weakens the emotional intensity connected to the memory without changing the memory itself. It just allows it to be "updated" so it feels less overwhelming while the facts remain intact.

Although this toolkit is still a work-in-progress, success stories have been recorded through the trial applications. One of such applications was on some folks whose traumatic experience was from romantic betrayal. They were all experiencing serious emotional distress before the trial. After the trial, about 80% of the 60 participants reported meaningful improvement in symptoms after two assessments and six therapy sessions.

Brunet shared that though it's an effective method that's proving to be more efficient than CBT, more work still needs to be done on it. Also, it's not a widespread tool that a lot of clinicians have mastery of, yet. Nevertheless, the breakthrough of this tool can enhance your ability to relive your memory without feeling any sting.

Repetition = Truth Illusion (Illusory Truth Effect)

The human mind is amazing and works in dynamic ways. People who understand the dynamics of this human faculty often master the art of swaying people. Little wonder some people faithfully believe and defend a belief system even if it is destructive.

One of the gates to your mind are your ears. The things you hear over and over again can sway you to believe in something even if it's not true. Even if that statement contradicts your values or beliefs, by being constantly exposed to it, your mind can become swayed to begin to accept it as the truth. That tells you how susceptible our minds are.

In their publication about illusory truth effects (Fazio et al. 2015) buttressed that most of the decisions we make daily are influenced by claims that aren't completely true. The authors added that the reason such ideas become influential over our choices is because of repetition. This is true because hearing the same statement over and over makes the brain start rating it as more believable than any new statement. The name for this cognitive phenomenon is the *illusory truth effect*.

According to (Hutchinson 2024), the illusory truth effect has a hold because the human brain inclines familiarity as a shorter route to determining what's true. So, whenever we hear something, our brain processes it and thinks something like, "I've heard this before, so it must be true." Hutchinson added that some studies have established that we sometimes don't need to hear a statement multiple times to believe it; just hearing it twice can sway our belief.

Do you now see why areas like advertising, journalism, politics, and social media have a strong sway on people's choices? The influencers in those fields also know that all they need to win people's hearts is to repeat their messages, whether they are true or not.

(Pilat and Krastev 2018) stated something more disturbing in their journal when they declared that a lot of people often pride themselves on being shielded against misinformation, but even the most knowledgeable people can fall for the illusory truth effect. They may doubt the verity of the false claim the first time they come across it, but by repeated exposure, they begin to think of it as true. Sadly, prior knowledge may not be strong enough to protect them against this shift in perception. This is one of the reasons why highly educated people make some decisions, based on some claims, that make you wonder why a person of such a class made such a weird decision.

Let's do a quick assessment here: Can a new habit be formed in 21 days?

I don't know about you, but somewhere in my subconscious, forming a new habit in 21 days is true. Why is it still there? I have read and heard it from some acclaimed behavioral gurus on the internet that new habits are formed within that period of time. This was even after I read elsewhere that the experiment conducted suggested that the timeline wasn't generic. It only applies in certain contexts, depending on the habits you want to form. However, I'd believed that 21-day suggestion to be true because it sounds plausible. So every time I want to take on new habits, it's the 21-day timeline in my subconscious that jumps at me first, not because it's universally correct, but because it's familiar.

Now, let's apply this same phenomenon and talk about traumatic memories. For someone who went through a painful experience, emotional imprints will be formed, and will keep replaying in their mind. Over time, the repeated mental replay of that memory will not only become familiar, but it'll also become definitive. It'll almost become their permanent truth that defines who they are, what they can expect from life, and how safe or unsafe the world is. So the more they recollect the memory, the more it influences their current choices even without being consciously aware.

In essence, you might avoid relationships because you know they'll end in betrayal. Where does this knowledge come from? Repeated mental replay of your past betrayal so frequently that it became your truth without exception. Is it because betrayal is inevitable? Not so, but because your mind has been inclined towards it from repeatedly rewatching pictures of betrayal from the past.

Why does someone believe that they're a failure no matter what they do? Echoes from past failures whisper to them from time to time that they're not capable until they accept it as their truth. Hence, they are shy to take opportunities even when they're the best in line to land it. That's an illusion, but it's their truth.

So here, I'd like you to reflect on this for a moment. Could it be that some of the beliefs guiding your choices, and that you hold on to as your truths, are just past painful memories that have been repeated in your mind so many times that they now influence your decisions today?

You might believe that you're not good enough. You may go along with a new relationship, yet subconsciously expect the sting of betrayal because you believe it's bound to happen. You believe that everyone is bound to leave you, and it's just a matter of time. You believe that you're insufficient. You believe that you don't deserve to be loved. You believe that no matter how good something sounds, it's bound to fail. You believe you can't amount to anything, no matter how much you try. You believe everyone who meets you is just out to take advantage of you. You believe all these to be true.

Why?

That's the only question I'm closing this chapter with: "Why?" Why do you believe what you believe about yourself to be true? If, after careful reflection, all the answers you could get are linked to an experience, you may want to query the truth of that experience and its influence over your present experiences.

Chapter Summary

- The human mind is vulnerable and flexible. It can be manipulated into believing what never happened as the truth, especially when it's trying to recall an experience that happened in the past. It's called false memory, and it can influence one's decision in the present.
- Some people don't truly leave the moment when a traumatic event happened; they keep reliving it in their present life like an event loop. Evidence of that is the effect the memory still has on them now whenever they recollect the memory.
- Mentally repeating the memory of a traumatic event in your mind can make you accept the experience as your truth. It can also influence your current choices, perception of self, and behavioral patterns, unless you start questioning it.

8

The Myth of 'Positive Thinking'

> Positive thinking is more than just a tagline. It changes the way we behave. And I firmly believe that when I am positive, it not only makes me better, but it also makes those around me better.
> —Harvey Mackay

In the mid-20th century, mainly around the 1940s and 1960s, a major wave of positive thinking swept through America. Norman Vincent Peale's bestseller, *The Power of Positive Thinking*, played a crucial role in this move. The idea of the "positive thinking" wave was to offer people a coping mechanism that would help them stay optimistic, avoid fear, and keep making progress despite the obvious threats to their well-being.

Did it work? Oh, yes, it did! It made a lot of sense to people. They had hope and had something to believe in. Workers adopted a cheerful, confident outlook to boost performance. Many had a reason to keep living.

However, how long did that last? Here's what happened:

- In trying to adopt a positive outlook, workers sometimes suppressed genuine struggles to "fit in" with the upbeat culture. The result? Emotional turmoil.
- Citizens were unable to express their emotional troubles, like sadness, doubt, or trauma, because the environment didn't support that. There couldn't be such negative energy in a highly upbeat society.
- Problems like PTSD from the war, poverty, and discrimination were often glossed over with slogans like "think positive". This left many folks feeling isolated.

The entire American culture during that period was defined by that wave. Yet, some people struggled with real problems that didn't get any real help, as they had few options to reach out because they could be seen as negative and unbelieving. So to flow with the trend, they committed themselves to thinking positively, too. Many held on to hope that they would get better. They believed that by releasing the energies of their positive thoughts towards their problems, they would be mysteriously solved and they would be free.

Did they get better? They became more frustrated. Some slid into depression. Some got tired of life and called it quits, sadly.

Now, here's the question: Is it wrong to think positively? I don't think so. But can it be harmful to shoehorn all your emotions into "positive thinking"? Definitely.

Toxic Positivity Defined

There's nothing wrong with being positive; in fact, we need to remain positive every day of our lives to do anything meaningful and progressive. However, when we ignore unpleasant emotions and treat them like they aren't there, that's playing a dangerous game we can't keep up for long. Eventually, those emotions will force themselves out whenever there's a crack in our positive thinking wall.

For better insight, what's toxic positivity? According to (Villines 2021), it demands positivity from people regardless of the challenges that they face, potentially silencing their emotions and deterring them from seeking social support. In a way, it's about suppressing your emotions to look fine on the outside. This doesn't help anyone's mental well-being.

(Cherry 2021) also added that aside from the outlook, the mindset is the real deal. People are encouraged to nurture a positive mindset, no matter how bad a situation may seem. Where's the harm in that? The harm there is when you're made to believe that having a positive mindset can't go with difficult emotions. It's either you embrace the mindset or be tormented by unpleasant emotions all your life. When both are optional and you have to choose one over the other. Obviously, no one would want to settle for the unpleasant option. So the scale tilts toward positive thinking.

Meanwhile, what many people don't realize is that those unpleasant emotions are products of unresolved issues. It could be trauma, stress, or recent setbacks. It might just even be a product of life's issues, nothing to worry about, but also not something to ignore. As long as these issues remain unresolved, no matter how much we try to ignore them and remain positive mentally, the underlying emotional feedback will keep popping up from time to time. Not even a positive mindset can stop it.

It's crucial to chip in here again that there's nothing wrong with having a positive outlook or mindset because it's really profitable for our mental well-being. However, like Cherry said, the main issue here is that life isn't always positive. At some point in time, we're confronted with some painful emotions due to some unpleasant events. When they happen, ignoring them isn't the right response to addressing them.

If you don't address them, they'll linger. They might disappear for a while, but they'll come back, and they'll keep returning to trouble you until you're able to address them headlong. Acknowledging them alone is a big step in addressing them. Processing them honestly is also crucial to accepting and improving your mental wellness.

Let me give an example of a professional, Tess. She was just laid off from a company she had served wholeheartedly for 9 years. As she stared at the letter in her hand, she felt like the rug had suddenly been pulled from under her. She thought of the bills piling up, her thin savings, and the fact that she had no idea where to go from there.

She mustered the courage to return home, putting on a smile. She tried to maintain that outlook for some days, but couldn't keep it up. The questions from friends and family made her spill the beans. Yet, despite opening up, the only thing she got from them was "Just stay positive". Some even tried to give her some hope that "Everything happens for a reason."

Although they meant well, they didn't offer her real help. Every time she heard such feedback, she felt more invisible. She needed more than what she was getting. She needed someone who would sit with her in her discomfort and acknowledge her fears and frustrations, not brush them aside with positivity.

Tess felt increasingly guilty and ashamed for feeling negative emotions, unlike others who were positive, but who weren't in her shoes to know what she was really struggling with. The constancy of the "be positive" message in the face of her inner turmoil led to self-criticism and harsh self-talk. This also affected her relationships and social dynamics, and her boyfriend broke up with her because, according to him, she was too "negative" and "didn't want to stay positive."

When your struggles are not acknowledged, you'll feel unseen, unheard, and unsupported. It makes you feel alone in the midst of a community of people. That form of isolation strains connections with others and affects your performance at work.

Here's another way to look at this: toxic positivity may make you feel like you're floating in the air with a positive mindset. It's all about good energy, no room for negative emotions. Yet, this mindset doesn't allow you access to the kind of genuine support you need when you're going through difficult times.

Here are a few ways toxic positivity manifests:

- Brushing off struggles with phrases like "just think positive" or "focus on the good."
- Invalidating feelings with "it could be worse".
- Pressuring people to hide unpleasant emotions to appear happy.

- Blaming individuals for their own unhappiness, whilst ignoring the situations that led to it.
- Overlooking systemic issues by urging positivity in the face of injustice.
- Shaming and judging others for expressing negative emotions.

So, basically, toxic positivity is about putting up a show, a facade, where you pretend to be happy when you're severely hurting within. That's psychologically dangerous. Little wonder people feel suffocated to the point they can't take it anymore, till they spontaneously flare up when triggered by slight issues, or even take their own lives. That kind of culture kills its own people. Positivity and acknowledging unpleasant emotions don't have to be alternatives.

Why the Brain Detects Fake Optimism

There's nothing wrong with being hopeful. In fact, hope is one of the most vital forces that keeps people moving forward when the road ahead is unclear. But when hope becomes exaggerated to the point that it ignores the reality of pain, the brain picks up on it instantly. You may not even realize it at first, but somewhere in the background, your mind is quietly rejecting the message. It knows when something does not feel emotionally true.

The human brain has a natural way of processing information that keeps us safe. One of its priorities is to notice anything that feels like a mismatch between what is being said and what is actually happening. When someone is going through something deeply painful and another person responds with a wave of optimism that feels too bright for the moment, the brain registers the difference. It can even trigger discomfort because there is an emotional gap between reality and the response.

Part of this comes from the way our brains have evolved. For thousands of years, people had to pay attention to threats to survive. This created a tendency to focus on unpleasant or dangerous information more than neutral or positive information. Psychologists sometimes call this the brain's negativity bias. It is not about being pessimistic; it is about being realistic enough to respond to actual danger. When someone tries to paint over a threatening or hurtful situation with forced positivity, the brain does not just ignore the threat. It resists the sugar-coated version of events.

Another reason the brain detects fake optimism is that it seeks emotional congruence. That means it wants the emotional tone of a message to match the reality it is experiencing. If you lose someone you love and a friend tells you to smile because they are in a better place, your brain does not find comfort in that statement. Instead, it might feel even more unsettled because your sadness is being met with something that does not acknowledge the depth of your loss.

Take Malik, for example. He had been working for months on a project he truly believed would get his small business noticed. On the day of his big pitch, the investor he was meeting with barely listened before rejecting him outright. Malik felt crushed. That night, when he told a friend what had happened, she smiled and said, "Cheer up, everything happens for a reason." She meant well, but Malik felt a wave of frustration. His mind was still replaying every detail of that meeting, every word the investor said, every moment where he wished he had done something differently. The comment about everything happening for a reason did not match his mental and emotional reality. His brain was still trying to make sense of what happened, and her words offered no space for that process.

In situations like this, the brain can even interpret forced optimism as a subtle form of invalidation. When a person's emotions are brushed aside in favor of a brighter narrative, it can create a sense of being unseen or unheard. That does more harm than good. Instead of reducing distress, it can add feelings of isolation, guilt, or shame for even having unpleasant emotions in the first place.

Fake optimism can also interfere with trust. When the words someone hears do not match their lived experience, they may start to question whether that person truly understands them. Over time, this weakens connections. In friendships, families, and workplaces, that gap can lead to withdrawal and a reluctance to open up again.

The good news is that the brain also responds well to realistic optimism. This is not about giving up hope, but about grounding hope in truth. It means you can say, "This is incredibly hard, and I am here with you," rather than pretending the pain does not exist. When someone hears words that match what they are feeling and still offer a path forward, the brain relaxes. There is no mismatch to resolve, no inner resistance to the message. Instead, the mind can focus on the possibility of healing without having to defend the validity of its own emotions.

This is why emotional honesty matters so much. When people try to meet suffering with nothing but sunshine, they risk creating the very disconnection they are trying to prevent. The brain knows when it is being asked to accept something that does not line up with reality. It resists not because it wants to stay in pain, but because it wants the truth to be acknowledged before moving on.

Realistic optimism respects that truth. It gives the brain the chance to process what has happened without feeling pressured to leap over the pain. It meets reality where it is and builds hope from there. And when hope is built on honesty, the brain does not reject it. It accepts it as something it can work with, something it can trust.

Suppression Rebound Effect

Have you ever tried to stop thinking about something but found out later that it keeps popping up in your mind instead of staying quiet? That experience offers a glimpse into what's known as the suppression rebound effect. It's a psychological term for describing our attempts to avoid certain thoughts, emotions, or memories, yet our efforts to suppress them only empower them to return stronger.

In doing this, elements of trauma may come back to cause PTSD and provide a base for its continuity (Davies and Clark 2025). Think of suppression this way: imagine a fence built to stop a flowing river. What do you think will happen in the long run if the river isn't channeled towards another course? The fence may hold for a while; however, the more the water keeps flowing towards that fence, the weaker the fence becomes. With time, the fence will give way, because the natural order for a river is to keep flowing. This is one of the things that has led to flooding in some nations of the world.

Similarly, when thoughts, emotions, or memories are suppressed without acknowledging them, the result will be mental chaos that can impact a person's entire well-being.

The first time psychologists studied suppression effects was in the late 1980s. Out of curiosity, Daniel Wegner, a Harvard social psychologist, wanted to know what would happen when people tried not to think about something. Through his *white-bear* experiment, he found out that the more the participants tried not to think about a white bear, the more the thought invaded their minds.

That's just an experiment to show what happens in reality because it does happen daily in real-life situations. A good example that you might be familiar with is what happens when a teenage girl's relationship breaks up. The usual procession of events is that her friends will rally round her, trash the guy who broke her heart, and encourage her along the lines of "Don't think about him. Just move on."

In taking that well-intentioned advice, she will most likely delete his photos, skip songs they both liked, and avoid places they used to visit. Yet, when she's alone, in those quiet moments, memories of him and moments they had together will creep back stronger than before.

She'll try to avoid the memories, but they will only drive her crazy, leading to her telling her friends, "I miss him. Can't I just give him a call?" to which their reply would be a chorused no. So, she'll keep trying not to think about him, but the very act of trying not to think about him will make her brain check in to see if the thought is gone. Doing so will bring the memories right back.

Whenever you tell yourself not to think about something, two processes are set in motion:

- The first is a conscious effort to distract yourself.
- The second is a subconscious monitoring system that keeps scanning for the forbidden thought to make sure it's not happening.

The rebound is in the second process because while you're monitoring, you're indirectly keeping the thought active. That will eventually create more mental space for the thought than it had before. That's why suppression rebound effects are often frustrating.

Suppression rebound doesn't apply to thoughts alone; it happens to emotions as well. When you tell yourself, "I won't feel anxious about tomorrow's meeting," that's when you'll notice you're giving more attention to anxiety. Once your brain heard the keyword "anxious", it flagged it as important, therefore making it more likely to come back.

While suppressing your thoughts may lead to frustration, emotional suppression can intensify distress. A study found that people who tried to suppress their emotions during a disturbing film not only reported feeling more stress, but they also showed greater physiological signs, like increased heart rate. When you suppress your emotions, they're hidden within your body, they don't show on your face. In essence, no one will notice anything. However, they would still remain in your body. As long as they're in your body, they can resurface with a greater force whenever they're triggered.

The rebound effect can also lead to unhealthy habits. For instance, smokers who tell themselves not to think about cigarettes may end up craving them more. Dieters who try to avoid thinking about chocolate often find themselves craving it until they eventually give in.

So why does the brain do this? Our minds don't respond well to negative commands. If someone tells you, "Don't think about pizza," your mind responds first by imagining pizza to understand what the person told you to avoid. The mental image of pizza will bring the unwanted thought to the front of your mind before you attempt to suppress it.

Another explanation comes from an area in psychology known as cognitive load. Suppression uses mental energy. The more stressed you are, the harder it becomes to maintain suppression, and the more likely the thought will bounce back with intensity.

I want you to understand that the suppression rebound effect isn't an academic exercise. It has a real-time impact on your mental well-being. That's why when people are grieving, for instance, a clinician or a therapist would counsel them to acknowledge and sit with their feelings because pushing them away will do a lot of harm to them. Then there's also the acceptance and commitment therapy (ACT) that teaches people to detach themselves from unwanted thoughts while they notice them without judging them. Then, in the same vein, they're taught to redirect their attention toward values-based actions. This approach reduces the struggle and prevents the rebound effect from taking over.

If you want to deal with this kind of issue in daily life, the key is to replace suppression with healthy engagement. If you're anxious about an upcoming event, acknowledge your feelings and prepare constructively rather than trying to erase the thought. Process any intruding memory instead of suppressing it. Journal it or talk it through with a friend you trust. By facing the thought, you give it less reason to hide in the shadows of your mind.

Emotional Agility Vs Emotional Denial

There was a time in the marketplace when intelligence quotient was what a lot of people rated as the criterion for being successful. However, as the world became even more sophisticated, custodians of the marketplace began to realize that IQ isn't enough. That's when talks about emotional intelligence (EI) became a thing, too.

Today, our world isn't getting less complex, even with the advancement in technology to make work processes easier. Responsibilities and demands of life are at an all-time high. EI is so crucial to handling all the challenges the present world throws at us. However, at the core of EI is something else, and that's what we want to focus on in this section.

Generally, life has its way of throwing diverse challenges that evoke different emotions in us. Some of them we embrace heartily, but some others we try to avoid. The way we respond to all of these emotions molds not only our mental health, but also the depth of our relationships and the authenticity of our lives.

Two common approaches often pop up during conversations about our emotional well-being. The first is **emotional agility**, and the second is **emotional denial.**

Do you think they seem related? Well, you're not the first to think so. However, in practice, they could not be more different.

I'll use this illustration to explain these concepts. Anita was a mid-level manager at a tech firm. For two years, she was overlooked for a promotion while some of her colleagues kept rising in the ranks. To look unconcerned before her colleagues, Anita would tell herself and them that "It is no big deal. I am fine." She looked cool with it. She would smile and even work late at night. Inwardly, resentment and bitterness were building.

She wasn't sleeping well anymore. Though she tried to push herself to work, she was feeling less motivated. That's emotional denial. She was refusing to acknowledge that disappointment and frustration were there. Instead of addressing them, Anita pushed them aside, hoping they'd disappear. However, suppressed emotions rarely vanish. They often resurface in ways we don't expect, sometimes as irritability, burnout, or even physical symptoms like headaches and fatigue.

Let's flip the story to reflect the other concept. Let's assume Anita still wasn't recognized for promotion, and instead of covering it up, she acknowledged the pain of being "ignored". To process her pain, she took a weekend off. During that weekend, Anita opened up to a trusted friend to talk about how she'd been feeling about the promotion. She identified what the experience meant to her and the value she placed on it in line with her career goals. What Anita would be doing that weekend would be engaging her emotions rather than denying them. That's what emotional agility is.

Emotional agility was first coined by a psychologist, Susan David, to mean the ability to use your emotions, with openness, curiosity, and compassion, to guide your choices based on your values (Bedsworth, 2022). It's not the same as controlling your emotions or trying to get rid of the unpleasant ones. Rather, you recognize them for what they are; you pay attention to the messages they convey; and based on what you learn, you make decisions that align with your values.

In essence, emotional agility is having an inner flexibility that lets you face hard truths and still move forward with clarity.

Emotional denial, on the other hand, is somewhat similar to suppression, and is actually a form of emotional suppression. However, one thing about this approach to emotion is that, according to Dean (2022), we often use it unconsciously as a defense mechanism to avoid uncomfortable emotions and tough circumstances. In essence, there's a way we unconsciously shut the door on certain emotions we aren't ready to feel.

It's almost like self-preservation; so you try to pretend that everything is fine when nothing is actually alright. In an ironic display, you can tell yourself, "I am not upset," yet, your jaw is clenched and you've been struggling to sleep. Emotional denial can feel like self-protection, but over time, it disconnects you from reality and from yourself. By refusing to acknowledge what you truly feel, you deny yourself the chance to process, heal, and grow.

Studies have shown that emotional suppression, which is the hallmark of emotional denial, can lead to increased physiological stress responses. As understanding increased in this field, it was linked to higher risks of anxiety, depression, and even cardiovascular issues (Richards & Gross, 2000). By contrast, emotional agility is associated with resilience, improved problem-solving, and higher overall life satisfaction (David & Congleton, 2013).

One of the main reasons emotional agility works better is that your emotions aren't random. They're data. For instance, anger signals that a boundary has been crossed. Sadness signals different things, but it could point to a loss that needs to be acknowledged. Anxiety often signifies uncertainty that we can prepare for. In other words, every time we deny these emotions, we ignore their messages. It's just like making serious efforts to turn off a smoke alarm when you're supposed to be putting out the fire.

Actually emotional denial often comes from good intentions, it's just simply trying to stay positive. However, like we discussed earlier, it's a toxic form of positivity. But true strength isn't the absence of emotion. It's the courage to face it and work with it constructively. This is why emotional agility doesn't mean wallowing in feelings forever. It means letting emotions pass through you like waves, not locking them in a closet.

So how do you build emotional agility? Take little steps like the ones highlighted below:

- Name what you are feeling without judgment. "I am feeling disappointed" is different from "I am a failure."
- Create space between you and your emotions so you can respond rather than react.
- Ask yourself, "What's this feeling trying to tell me?" and "What action aligns with my values here?"

Practice and practice some more. The more you do, you'll begin to realize that your emotions aren't your enemies but guides trying to tell you something.

The "Both/And" Brain

With all my years of interacting with people, I can say for a fact that humans are one complex creature. One of the things that amps up this complexity is our emotions. Honestly, we may think that we have a handle on how to describe our emotions, but in reality, they're often more layered than the words we use to describe them. Or how else will you describe feeling seemingly opposite emotions at the same time? For want of adequate expression, psychologists call it mixed emotions. This phenomenon describes the occurrence where you can hold both positive and negative emotions together, like happiness and sadness at the same time.

Due to the complexity of our brains, too, you can't limit it to a binary thinking pattern such as "either/or". So, don't expect your brain to only see things through a black and white lens. Its inclination is more towards a "both/and" pattern. What this means is that our brains have the capacity to hold opposite emotions at the same time. You can feel grateful and sad. You can be excited and anxious. You can love someone deeply and still feel frustrated with them.

Contrary to what you might be thinking, this isn't an error in your brain wiring. In fact, it's one of your brain's strengths. We need to maximize it for your well-being.

Some psychologists discovered that emotional complexity is actually a sign of maturity and resilience. It reflects the brain's ability to integrate different pieces of reality rather than forcing a false choice. Grühn et al. (2013) shared that there are people who feel multiple emotions at once. Not only that, they can also tell apart the subtle differences between what they feel, recognize how their emotions differ from those of others, and give expression to a wide range of feelings. That's what emotional complexity entails. They also affirmed that it's a key marker of healthy emotion regulation and overall mental well-being in adulthood.

Research in affective neuroscience suggests that when people experience mixed emotions, it helps them cope better with changes and uncertainties. In essence, when someone experiences happiness and sadness together, they will be better able to process their endings and transitions in a healthy way.

It's just like a student graduating from the university. On one hand, they feel immense pride in what they achieved while studying. They'll also be excited about what the future holds for them. However, on the other hand, they would be feeling sad. Do you know why? They're about to leave their friends behind. Also, they feel concerned about going into an unpredictable job market. If they tried to suppress one side of that experience, they might lose the richness of the moment and reduce their capacity to adapt. It's only by acknowledging both experiences that they'd be able to process their change and transitions totally.

What this means is that the "both/and" brain thinking pattern is especially important when dealing with life's challenges. Many people think that if they're going through a hard time, they must wait until they're fully "over it" before they can experience joy again. In reality, the brain can access joy and pain side by side.

You might be grieving a loss and still find yourself laughing at a funny memory. Haven't you experienced that before? You might be anxious about a medical diagnosis but also deeply appreciative of the support you're receiving from loved ones.

This dual capacity isn't about pretending things are fine when they're not. What you're doing instead is creating space for the whole spectrum of your emotions without making one to cancel the other. Remember, each emotion is sending a message across.

In propagating emotional agility, Susan David explained that when you reject certain emotions or you force yourself to choose between emotions, it often leads to emotional rigidity. The best approach is to be curious about your emotions and learn from them without judging them.

A common misunderstanding is that embracing both sides will make us "weak" or indecisive. That's not true. It doesn't weaken, rather it strengthens your psychological flexibility. With this level of flexibility, you'll be able to adapt your responses based on context instead of being trapped in a distorted thinking like all-or-nothing thinking. From a neurological perspective, it engages multiple regions of the brain, including the prefrontal cortex, which is linked to complex reasoning and decision making.

Both/and brain can also enhance your relationships. When you recognize that you can love someone and be angry with them at the same time, you'll be free and open to communicate more honestly with them, without feeling that one emotion must cancel the other. This way, it'll be easier to resolve conflicts and maintain trust.

Taking the same to your workplace, leaders who can acknowledge both the challenges and the opportunities in a situation are more likely to inspire more confidence than those who insist on relentless positivity; the toxic type of positivity.

The "both/and" brain also helps us navigate moral and ethical complexity. Life is rarely made up of clear heroes and villains. We often encounter situations where good people make mistakes or where solutions carry both benefits and costs. The ability to hold contradictory truths allows for more empathy and better problem solving.

However, living with this awareness can be uncomfortable because our brains naturally seek certainty. It's easier to pick one side and stick with it. However, growth often requires tolerating discomfort.

Ultimately, the "both/and" brain is a reminder that life isn't rolled out as a smooth sequence of separate emotional states. It's a layered experience where joy and sorrow, hope and fear, strength and vulnerability can coexist. Recognising and embracing this complexity isn't a sign of confusion. It's a sign of wisdom.

If we allow ourselves to live in the "both/and" space, we don't just survive life's contradictions. We thrive in them. We stop waiting for perfect conditions to feel whole and instead learn to carry our wholeness into imperfect moments. That's the kind of emotional strength that carries us through change, connects us to others, and deepens our humanity.

Chapter Summary

- In a period when period desperately seeks hope and assurance of good days ahead, positivity becomes a strength. However, when it's embraced at the cost of real emotional pain, it becomes toxic. Yet, instead of making positivity and experiencing emotional pains alternatives, both can work together for a healthier well-being.
- Suppressing emotions is as dangerous as blocking the path of a flowing stream without creating another channel for it. While the emotions can appear tamed initially, they'll eventually blow in your face beyond what you can handle whenever they're triggered.
- With emotional agility, you'll learn to listen to your emotions because they're couriers that bear specific messages. In essence, unpleasant emotions are only unpleasant because of

how they make you feel. However, when you learn to sit with them and experience them, instead of denying them, you'll realize that there's more you can learn from them to enhance your living.

PART 3

Breaking Free

The sound of freedom is often filled with hope and positivity. Yet, throughout human history, no true freedom from oppressive control was without some form of effort. Similarly, there can't be true freedom from the hold of old narratives without some form of effort from you.

As we move towards the concluding part of this journey, I invite you to brace up as we delve into insights about the field of battle and strategies for acquiring true emotional and mental freedom.

The extent of your freedom is dependent on your commitment. Ready to put in some fight? Let's get you equipped then!

PART 3

Breaking free

9

The 90-Second Rule

> It is a choice. No matter how frustrating or boring or constraining or painful or oppressive our experience, we can always choose how we respond.
> – Edith Eger

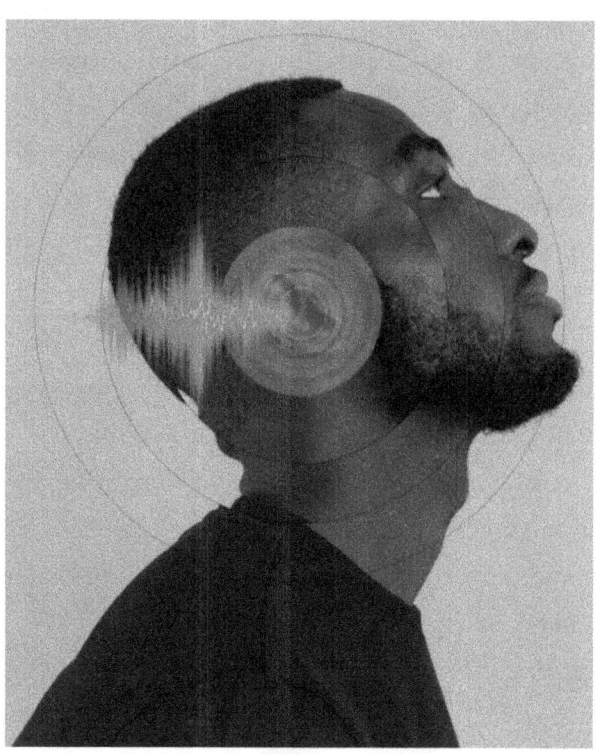

The Emotional Wave Theory

Have you noticed that your emotions don't move in straight, predictable lines? They're more like an oceanic wave that rises and falls without a definite pattern. Sometimes, they can be gentle, while they can be boisterous at other times. However, one thing is certain, like an ocean, they're always in motion. This is the importance of the Emotional Wave Theory.

This theory refers to the dynamism of emotions. They are also cyclical. But they're never in a fixed state. Our emotions have a natural rhythm of building, peaking, and subsiding. It's only when we're able to understand this rhythmic flow that we can ride on our emotional waves with stability, rather than feeling crushed by them.

Another way to put it is that in their true form, emotions are energy in motion. Taking a look at the root word of emotion—*emovere* (Latin)—it means "to move out." Hence, they're never known to be static. In studying and describing emotions, neuroscientists call emotions a complex reaction involving the brain and the body. This interaction often triggers chemical changes, physiological responses, and behavioral impulses.

If you're familiar with oceanic waves, you'd know that they're transient. They're not the normal current of an ocean. This implies that they have a lifespan. During this time frame, they intensify, reach a crest, and subside. That's almost how emotional waves operate, too. When they hit, they intensify, and eventually subside.

From the way I describe this emotional wave, it seems they come and go without hassle. However, is that our true experiences? Most times, no! The real problem with these waves is in our response to them. Whenever we try to resist or freeze a wave mid-crest, we'll have some difficulties.

It's usually exhausting, isn't it? Compare resisting or freezing an emotional wave with trying to stand in the ocean and try to hold a wave in place with your hands. Isn't that suicidal itself? Yet that's what happens every time we make efforts to suppress emotions or cling to them. So, instead of moving naturally, they either crash harder later or get stuck. Eventually, they'll create a kind of emotional undertow.

One of the powerful facts the Emotional Wave Theory establishes is that no emotion, no matter how intense, lasts forever. The creator of Dialectical Behavior Therapy (DBT), Psychologist Marsha Linehan, once stated that most intense emotions reach their climax and begin to subside within 90 seconds to a few minutes. However, that's if we let them run their normal course without feeding them with rumination or resistance. In essence, when you're in the middle of an emotional surge, don't rush to quell them instantly for whatever reason. Rather, stay grounded long enough for the wave to pass.

I once read about a young professional woman, Meg (not real name), who was criticized by her manager during a team meeting. In that context, the spontaneous emotional wave that hit her first was a mix of embarrassment and defensiveness. Her heart rate shot up. Her face flushed. Her mind raced in all directions to gather counterarguments. However, anyone who knew Meg in the past would know that she's slower in her reaction than usual. Her former self would have given a sharp and quick response in anger or quiet treatment.

Though it made her look smart, it wasn't great for her reputation. It wasn't good for her relationships either. Hence, over time, she had to learn to understand her emotional wave patterns. In response to them, Meg chose pause as a better course of action. Like in this context, though embarrassed, she focused on her breath, and took some notes to extract the facts from the manager's criticism. Finally, she wasn't in a rush to exit the meeting venue when it ended. She stayed back to process the entire experience. Within 10 minutes, that wave began to dissipate. When she scheduled a follow-up conversation with her manager, she approached the issue with curiosity rather than attack. The result was a productive dialogue instead of a relationship rupture.

One of the things we can deduce from Meg's experience is that the Emotional Wave Theory also has profound implications for relationships. When you understand that your partner's anger or sadness is part of a passing wave, you're less likely to take it personally. You won't escalate it out of proportion in response. Hence, this encourages patience and empathy. However, it's a two-way street, and most crucial of all is that you need to recognize that your own frustration or fear is a wave that can prevent you from making permanent decisions in temporary states.

Another important fact I'd like to point out is that not all waves are negative. Joy, excitement, and inspiration are all positive emotions that follow a rise-and-fall pattern too. Have you ever felt let down after a big positive event? It's not just your experience. That phenomenon is known as the "post-achievement slump." It's not a sign that the positive feeling you felt earlier wasn't real. It was! Why you felt the way you did afterward is because joy, and all other positive emotions, also follow the rhythmic pattern of an emotional wave. They rise and fall. When you understand this, you'll savor those high moments without clinging to them desperately. Also, you won't panic when they fade.

Whenever you try to resist the natural rhythm of emotional waves, it often leads to burnout and emotional numbness. If you've ever felt "stuck" in sadness or stress for weeks, it's often because the wave is being blocked by unprocessed grief, unacknowledged anger, or chronic overthinking. Through systems like therapy, journaling, and safe conversations, you can help unblock these waves and let them move again.

Emotional Rumination Vs Processing

Many of us have lived life long enough to know that life isn't a bed of roses. It's laced with thorns and thistles, yet it's a beautiful privilege to be given an opportunity to live purposefully. The challenges we face daily seem to be integrated into the curriculum of our short stint on earth. This means that none of us is without a form of challenge at different phases of our lives.

Although challenges are common to all, our approach to them is what distinguishes us apart from one another. Generally, there are two approaches to how people handle challenges:

- Rumination
- Processing

Zofkie (2024) compared rumination to being stuck on a mental hamster wheel. Instead of moving forward, you're constantly revisiting specific thoughts or situations. You can consider it as a repetitive cycle that involves overthinking and analyzing. While you may mistake it for trying to process your thoughts, it's actually leaning you into emotional distress.

Ruminating is an act of replaying past events in your mind, worrying about the future outcomes, or fixating on the perceived mistakes. There's just one thing that makes this exercise futile and harmful, there's no guarantee of getting a solution. When we ruminate, our mind drifts off to terrains we don't have control over and we even worry about them. We were stopped from meeting a deadline because of an unforeseen heavy snowing yesterday, yet we're worried the weather the next day will hinder us from doing anything significant. Then we begin to worry about a potential futile day, bla bla bla. With all those worrying, there's no real progress because we won't be able to see the opportunity in the challenges.

Most times, our minds latch at the challenges life throws at us. When we do, we keep thinking about the same hurtful moments, awkward conversations, or unfair situations over and over again. Once you indulge that trend of thinking, it often never seems to stop playing.

Matey (2023) stated that rumination is like doing a recycling trade of thoughts. However, instead of coming up with great outcomes, we never come to a conclusion after recycling the thoughts multiple times. Instead, we either end up anxious or depressed. When we remunerate, we focus on "why" in an unproductive way. It's like having a song stuck in your head, except the song is made of your own worries and frustrations.

Therefore, the characteristics of emotional rumination are:

- Repetitive Thinking
- Focus on Negative Aspects
- Lack of Resolution
- Increased Stress

The other approach is emotional processing. This approach may start off like rumination, but it doesn't end like it because it's a more constructive and purposeful way of interacting with thoughts and emotions (Zofkie, 2024). When we process our thoughts, we're actively making efforts to carefully examine them from different angles before coming up with a solution. Hence, you don't get stuck with the approach, you advance with more clarity and confidence.

With emotional processing, you're able to engage with your emotions intentionally. You will be able to acknowledge them fully and seek meaning in a way that helps you move forward. Thus, instead of spinning your wheels, you're steering the car. While processing your thoughts or emotions, you can ask questions like:

"What is this feeling trying to tell me?"

"What is within my control to change here?"

The key characteristics of emotional processing are:

- Active Engagement
- Balanced Perspective
- Goal-Oriented
- Emotional Growth

While you face the risk of depression, prolonged negative moves, and heightened feelings of helplessness while ruminating, you'll become more resilient, solve problems better, and develop strong immunal functions through emotional processing.

The brain responds differently to each. During rumination, the brain's default mode network is activated. This network is linked to self-referential thinking. Stay long with the thought and you'll remain stuck in a loop. However, emotional processing engages areas linked to problem-solving and emotional regulation, like the prefrontal cortex. A transition from one of these to the other can change how we feel and even how our bodies respond to stress.

While trying to exercise emotional processing, avoid thinking that processing is about rushing to make yourself feel better almost immediately. You would have missed the essence of this exercise because in reality, it's about making space for the full truth of our emotions while still moving progress in your healing experience. Psychologist Guy Winch often says that people should treat emotional injuries the way they treat physical ones. Even though they can heal themselves, they'll be prolonged. Emotional healings are like that, too. They'll take longer to heal if we keep ignoring them.

Let's talk about how to practice processing instead of ruminating. Here are a few practical things you can try:

- Set aside a specific "worry time" during the day to think about the situation. This contains the mental loop rather than letting it run all day.
- Write about what happened for 15 minutes, focusing on your feelings, your thoughts, and possible ways forward.
- Talk it through with someone who can help you clarify your thoughts rather than fuel the negativity.

With time, you can train your brain to identify when you're circling the same thought without progress. That awareness is the first step toward breaking the cycle.

In summary, rumination can look like sitting in a rocking chair. It feels like you have something to do, but it's actually moving nowhere. However, processing is equivalent to actually walking down a path. Though you may still feel the weight of the emotions, You may still feel the weight of your emotions, but you're purposefully making progress towards healing.

The Cortisol Hangover

Have you ever wondered why you feel so drained long after an emotionally intense moment has passed? It's not just something you thought of in your head. Your body is actually feeling it. What that means is that your body is trying to process the chemical aftermath of the experience. It's like having a hangover after a party ended hours ago. For the body, it's not intoxication from drinks that's responsible for the hangover, it's an element in the body called cortisol.

Cortisol is the body's main stress hormone. It's often released whenever your brain registers a threat, whether the threat is real, imagined, or just anticipated. When this hormone is released, your heart rate rises, your breathing changes, your muscles tighten, and you're suddenly ready for fight, flight, or freeze. It's an ancient survival system that worked well when danger meant outrunning a predator. However, in modern life, that same system can be triggered by an email from your boss. It could even be an argument with a loved one.

When you have a cortisol hangover, you'll feel your body is still not balanced after an emotional wave just passed. Your thoughts may have moved on, but your nervous system is still simmering. This is why you might still feel heavy, unmotivated, or even tense when you wake up the next morning after an event, like an intense fight, took place. This doesn't happen because you're having a sort of weakness. It's biological.

Cortisol doesn't go away after the problem is over. It hangs around in your system. It keeps your body in a slightly heightened state of alertness.

However, things get mixed up when you begin to take how you feel as the truth. In essence, emotional intensity isn't the same as emotional truth. When your cortisol is high, your feelings can look absolute than they are.

For instance, the harsh text message you got from your friend might feel like a proof that they no longer value you. Yet in reality, they typed that message in haste because they were in the middle of a busy day, yet they knew they still had to respond. There are many other examples like that.

This is to tell you that the story floating freely in your mind while you're in the midst of a heated stress isn't always accurate. However, most times, your body convinces you that it's because the physical sensations are so strong. Being able to know the difference between what you feel and the truth helps you to build emotional resilience. You'll understand that your feelings when in the middle of a stress spree aren't often the same when your system is calm.

Sadly, when we resist emotions, we often make the hangover worse. Many people try to outrun uncomfortable feelings by numbing out with food, social media, work, or endless distractions. But unprocessed emotions do not dissolve. They wait. Pushing them away simply adds more tension to an already taxed nervous system. You may think you are coping, but your body is still holding the charge of that unacknowledged emotion, which prolongs the hangover effect.

The key to breaking the cycle is to meet the emotion rather than resist it. This doesn't mean you wallow in it or magnify it. It means you notice it without judgment, you name it for what it is, and you give your body the signal that it's safe to let go. Something as simple as slow, deep breathing can help lower cortisol and shift your body toward a calmer state.

Movement helps too, something like a short walk, stretching, or even shaking out your limbs can literally help discharge some of the tension. Sometimes, just speaking out loud to yourself with a phrase like "This was a hard moment, and my body is still coming down from it" can break the spell of emotional intensity.

I once worked with someone who had frequent clashes with her team. Every heated meeting left her feeling drained for the rest of the day and sometimes into the next. She thought she was simply bad at managing conflict. In reality, she was stuck in a cycle of cortisol hangovers. The arguments triggered her stress response, her body flooded with cortisol, and even after the conversation ended, she stayed in fight-or-flight mode. The turning point came when she started practicing what I call a pause ritual. After a tense meeting, she would step outside, breathe slowly for two minutes, and do a mental check-in to remind herself the danger had passed. Over time, the hangovers shortened because her body learned how to downshift more quickly.

If you have ever noticed that your mood feels "off" long after the trigger event, you're likely experiencing the same thing. You're not overreacting. Your nervous system is simply completing a chemical cycle, and your job is to support it rather than sabotage it. That means giving yourself recovery space instead of pushing through as if nothing happened. It means questioning the first, most intense interpretation of events instead of accepting it as the full truth. Also, it means remembering that emotions are not a threat to be conquered but waves to be ridden with skill.

When you stop resisting emotions, something interesting happens. They move. They lose their grip. The cortisol still runs its course, but without the extra layer of tension that comes from fighting yourself. You recover faster, and you emerge clearer. That's the difference between living at the mercy of your stress chemistry and learning to work with it.

The cortisol hangover isn't a personal flaw. It's a natural human response to emotional intensity. But once you understand it, you are no longer powerless to it. You can interrupt the cycle, you can see through the false urgency of heightened feelings, and you can allow your emotions to pass without letting them set up camp in your body. That is what it means to live with emotional wisdom.

Practicing the Pause

Just imagine what will happen if you take a pause before you actually react angrily. You'll feel more in control and be able to weigh your options before you react. That's the kind of power you have when you pause.

There's a quiet power in learning to pause before reacting. But you know, "fast" is the name of the game in the digital age, right? Virtually everything and everyone is aiming to get faster, because it seems that the only way we don't get left behind. However, did you know the human brain was not designed to thrive in constant acceleration? When we're faced with emotionally charged situations, our nervous system is the first to react. The amygdala sends signals that prepare the body for fight, flight or freeze. Our heart rate increases, adrenaline floods the bloodstream, and cortisol surges. When all these start to take place, we're being prepped for action, not reflection. Here's why the pause is so important. The pause is the space between stimulus and response. That's where you can make your choice instead of being driven by automatic reaction.

Pausing isn't the same as ignoring your emotions; it's not pretending that it isn't there either. It's just that despite being aware of its presence, you're giving the prefrontal cortex of your brain, where thinking takes place, enough room to breathe and intervene. I want you to know for a fact that there's truly a space between your stimulus and response. It's in that space that your power and freedom lies.

Just a few seconds of conscious pause can reduce the intensity of your emotional reactivity and increase your chance to decide. It also allows you to notice what's going on in your body and mind. That's the point where you'll feel the heat rising, the tension in your chest, and the tightening in your jaw. Pausing is a skillful response, and the first step to making a conscious choice.

Let's imagine a parent struggling to deal with a child's tantrum. Without the pause, they'll always feel frustrated, vent, and punish the child more than guiding the child. However, with the pause, they can breathe, ground themselves, and focus more on teaching the child, not stamping their authority on the child forcefully.

Similarly, an employee who's been getting critical feedback in meetings can do better with a pause, than without it. They'd be more defensive, take offense, argue more, or even shut down without a pause. However, with a pause, they'll get more feedback, ask questions for clarification, and respond constructively. What's the difference? The space, not the situation.

A pause can be as short as three deep breaths. It can also be as long as a walk around the block. What really matters isn't the duration but the intention behind it. Every time you pause in such stressful situations, you're signalling to your brain and body that it's safe to step out of survival mode. Your Cortisol levels will begin to stabilize afterwards and your nervous system will start shifting toward a calmer state. This shift makes it easier to think clearly, to weigh options, and to communicate in ways that keep relationships rather than damage them. With time, the more you practice pause, the more your stress response gets rewired. You'll become less reactive and more intentional.

Pausing also helps you break free from the false urgency that modern life imposes. Not every email needs an instant reply. Not every disagreement needs to be settled in the heat of the moment. When you pause, you're reminded that you have time to reflect, understand the context, and match your response with your values. Patience will become your active choice, not a passive state. You'll know the importance of this as you practice it in situations like an emotionally charged conversation, where words spoken in haste can cause lasting harm.

Pause can take many forms. Below are some common practices that you can adopt, or combine to make yours:

- A physical cue like placing one hand on your chest to anchor yourself in the present.
- Repeating a phrase like "This can wait" or "Breathe first."
- Counting to ten before reacting.
- Taking a sip of water.
- Asking for a moment to think.

In all, the objective isn't emotional suppression but leverage to give you more clarity. Even when emotions are intense, pausing can help you identify what feels urgent in the moment might not be as critical once the initial rush passes.

This habit becomes even more powerful when paired with self-compassion. Sometimes we react before we remember to pause, and that's part of being human. The point is to keep practicing. With time, the brain will learn that a pause isn't a delay in action but a step toward wiser action. As simple as this is, it can protect your relationships, support better decisions, and preserve your emotional energy.

Although pausing might feel counterintuitive at first in a culture that often equates speed with competence, the evidence is clear. People who master the pause often have greater influence, stronger relationships, and better resilience in the face of stress.

Pausing isn't about inaction. It's choosing the right action at the right time for the right reason. It's about showing up in a way that aligns with your values and the person you want to be, rather than being driven by how you're feeling in the moment. Eventually, pausing isn't just a technique, it's how you reclaim your power from impulse and give it back to intention.

Chapter Summary

- Emotional rumination often feels like you're actually processing your thoughts and emotion, but the eventual outcome often shows that you've just been going in a circle that sinks you deeper in negativity and pessimism, rather than taking meaningful actions.
- Cortisol is a natural body response to stress, resisting the emotions isn't. When you resist the emotion, you're putting yourself at the mercy of your stress to make you feel tense and put you on the edge. However, learning to notice it without judgment, naming it for what it is, will give your body the signal that it's safe to let go. That's healthier.
- As simple as a pause is, it has the power to give you a lever in an emotionally intense situation. Instead of being driven hard by emotional surges, you'll have a handle to hold, to stabilize you and allow you to make intentional decisions.

10

Rewriting Your Mental Code

> Our brains are plastic, and we have the ability to change and shape them throughout our entire lives.
> —Andrew Huberman

How would you feel if you knew that you can do so much more with your brain than you're currently doing? This revelation could be the turning point in your life. Perhaps you think your life is predictable, that could be because you've not flexed your brain enough to reframe your thoughts, chart new territories, or explore new possibilities beyond what you experienced in the past. If you could do any of these, your life will experience an unimaginable shift that will daze you too.

Why would any change in the brain reshape your entire life? Simply put, your brain is the director of your life's affairs, these include your thoughts, emotions, and behavioral patterns. At its core, the way your brain is wired influences everything you do daily. Hence, if your brain is wired to be fearful, you'll always think fear, act fearfully, and believe fear. This—fear—in itself is the definition of some people's daily experience. Everyone is wired differently, but the main thing to know is that our lives are reflections of how we've been wired.

One question that might be running through your mind is, who did the wiring? In reality, no one deliberately sits down to be wired to fear. In fact, when we were all born, we came clean, however, our experiences and exposure to certain environments shaped our brains to think, feel, and behave in certain ways.

For one, experiences are a powerful determinant of our brain's wiring. For most people reading this book, this is true. Many of those experiences weren't our doing, circumstances warranted them. For instance, someone who was betrayed by someone they loved could become traumatic from that experience—one they didn't prepare for. However, after that first experience, they may be inclined to expect betrayal in any other love relationship, thereby wiring their brain not to fully trust their partners.

The essence of this chapter is to let you know that your life isn't cast in stones. Your brain is so dynamic that it can be rewired to adopt new ways of thinking, feeling, and behaving. That's leverage! Meaning, you can expose your mind to things that will reshape it in order to give you the kind of experiences you desire daily. This also gives you the power to be the primary determiner of your experiences, not other people's choices or actions.

I dare say that this is your ticket to independence. It's being free from being controlled by your past and the effects of other people's choices or actions on you. This is a pathway to unboxing and experiencing a side of you that you've always yearned for.

Let's unbox together!

What is Neuroplasticity?

Of all the parts of the human body, the brain is often described as the most complex organ, this is for good reason. As a result, it's a part that's still being studied and understood. Some centuries ago, a lot of scientists believed and propagated that the structure of the human brain becomes fixed and unchangeable once a person reaches adulthood. In fact, there was this conference where someone confidently said that anyone who wants to experience transformation in their lives must do it while they're still young because it's quite impossible for anyone to change in their adulthood. It sounded plausible, but it's not the entire truth.

Those who believed that notion taught that we all came into this world with a certain number of brain cells and wiring patterns. As we grow older, those connections become weaker or die off. However, as knowledge increased in this field, modern neuroscientists began to question that earlier notion about the brain.

The outcome of that continuous querying is that today we know that the brain isn't static but dynamic. We now know that the brain has the capability to constantly reshape and reorganize itself in response to experiences, choices, and environments. This ability is what is now known as neuroplasticity.

Puderbaugh and Emmady (2023) described neuroplasticity, or neural plasticity, as a process in which the brain goes through adaptive structural and functional changes. They added that this change often happens in response to intrinsic or extrinsic stimuli. When the change is ongoing, the brain is reorganizing its structure, functions, or connections. When these changes are ongoing, it's the brain's neurons, or nerve cells, that are changing (Cherry, 2024).

In essence, neuroplasticity is what makes structural and functional changes to happen in your life. Have you ever seen where a potter is shaping a piece of clay into something new? That's what happens to the brain. It rewires itself by strengthening certain pathways while letting others fade. The reason why you can learn new skills, adapt after injury, change long-standing habits, or change a thought pattern is because of neuroplasticity.

Do you remember the first time you rode a bicycle? Everything might feel clumsy initially. One of the things you had to learn to do was balancing while you're pedaling, then there's steering. You might not master all these on the first day, but with practice, your brain builds stronger connections between the neurons involved in those movements. What you'll realize afterwards is that riding becomes second nature. That's neuroplasticity!

Repetition wouldn't have been a necessary skill when learning something new, but to form stronger connections between the neurons involved and the new thing, you need to repeat it a couple of times. Every time we practice something, we're strengthening the neural connections that support it. Also, we're creating the pathway to be smoother and more efficient.

Neuroplasticity isn't only about learning new things, it also enhances recovery. That was why Puderbaugh and Emmady made reference to stroke and traumatic brain injury (TBI) as examples of conditions that neuroplasticity can have some influence on.

A stroke patient who loses their mobility on one side of their body can regain the ability to walk again or use their hands again through consistent therapy. Their brain will form new pathways around the damaged areas to cover up for the lost function. By implication, even after a part of the brain suffers injury, it can adapt, reassign tasks, and restore movement or language skills.

Sometime ago, Eleanor Maguire and her research team conducted a study to uncover the brain's flexibility. Their case study were London taxi drivers who had to memorize the city's complex network of streets. In their finding, they discovered that these drivers have larger hippocampi, that's the part of the brain related to spatial navigation. They weren't born like that, however with use, that part grew larger. This research proved that the brain can physically change in response to mental demands. Areas that are heavily used have the tendency to grow.

Through neuroplasticity, you can change the way you respond to the challenges you face. If you've been living with anxiety for many years, the fact is that your anxious response is beyond psychological; it is deeply encoded in your neural circuits. Through experiences, your brain has learned how to power certain pathways whenever it perceives threat. The good thing is that you can create new pathways to regulate our stress responses better. With the right tools and time, your old anxiety-driven pathways will grow weaker, while the new ones will become healthier. Hence, neuroplasticity is multi-dimensional in its function. It's not limited to skills development. It's capable of changing a lot of things about you.

With this brain's capability, we know that it's possible for anyone to change, this includes areas where they might feel stuck. With consistent effort, long-term habits and behavioral patterns can be rewired. That's why counselors or therapists often encourage their patients to practice journaling, cognitive reframing, or meditation continuously. Those exercises can literally reshape the brain over time.

It may interest you to know that this same ability to unlearn and learn new positive habits can also be used to strengthen harmful patterns if no caution is taken. Pessimism isn't a function of a one-time thinking, it was reinforced by dwelling on negative thoughts. Once that pathway becomes strengthened, pessimism will become the default response. This goes for addictive behaviors too. What those behavioral patterns do is to hijack the brain's reward system to create strong neural loops which makes it difficult to break free. What I'm trying to establish here is that neuroplasticity is neutral. It enhances whatever you repeatedly do—healthy or destructive practices.

What this implies is that your experience hereon is dependent on your daily actions. Your brain is listening to the instructions you're giving it through your choices and routines. Either you're trying to learn a new language, practice gratitude, or just learning to focus better, your brain is learning and forming new pathways. This process is similar to when you're trying to exercise your body to build muscles. Neuroplascticity is proof that your mind can build stronger neural connections as well.

What pathways do you want to strengthen?

Hebb's Law and Habit Formation

"Cells that fire together wire together."

The quote above is attributed to a Canadian psychologist named Donald Hebb. In his illustrious lifetime, he devoted his energy to studying human behavioral patterns. That quote was one of the outcomes of his relentless study. Hebb's idea about cells that fire together wire together became one of the most quoted laws in neuroscience because of its profoundness. That idea is also the core of what is known as Hebb's Law.

What Hebbs was saying with that rule is that the brain can strengthen the connections between neurons when they're set in motion almost at the same time. In essence, he's saying two or more neurons are better than one working alone. Hence, every time two or more neurons fire together, they form connections which likely grow stronger. With time, it'll become easier to activate them together later on. According to Hebb, that's the foundation for habit formation.

In applying Hebb's law to her Sensory Integration work, Beins (2022) explained that to get a sense actively strong, pair it with the senses that are actively working. Then use the strong senses to carry the seemingly inactive sense along. Let's assume that you're learning to play a musical instrument. Every note might feel awkward at first. Your fingers may fumble on the piano's keys. However, with practice, every neuron responsible for those movements will begin to fire together more consistently.

A more practical example is this: let's say you're trying to make a habit of making your bed daily but you keep failing at it, you could connect making your bed to another action you do regularly, let's say putting on your shoes. Hence, to strengthen your ability to make your bed regularly, do it when you're putting on your shoe. That's what Hebbs is saying.

What strengthens the neural circuits isn't the one-time pairing, but repeated pairing. Before you realize it, what you couldn't do well when you started will become smooth, or almost automatic activity for you. That's what every kind of habit—good or bad—is built on. Like neuroplasticity, this principle is neutral. However, you can use it to enhance your well-being.

There may be nothing automatic about reaching for a cup of coffee first thing in the morning. However, if you continue doing it, the cells associated with waking up, walking to the kitchen, and brewing coffee begin to fire together regularly. Keep at it and the connection will grow stronger until it becomes your default mode daily. At that point, you won't need much conscious effort to brew coffee first thing in the morning. Hence, Hebb's rule made it obvious that a repeated action can become an ingrained habit.

Hebb's law also explains why certain habits feel difficult to break. Long-standing habits are an indication that the neurons firing together to strengthen that habit are deeply entrenched. Let's say someone smokes a cigarette whenever they're stressed to get some relief, the brain will strengthen the connection between stress relief and nicotine. As this continues, this pathway will become the brain's automatic response to stress.

One will need more than just resisting the old pathway to break that habit. One would have to build a new pathway different from the former. The neurons must be re-trained to fire in different pairs, thereby creating new associations. Exercise could be a replacement for smoking as a stress response. Hence, the repeated combination of movement with relief will form a new habit gradually.

Hebb's Law can also be applied to thought patterns. If you repeatedly entertain negative self-talk, like "I will never succeed," whenever you experience a setback, the neurons in charge will fire together and strengthen that loop. The frequency at which you repeat it will determine if it'll become your default thought pattern. However, if you consistently practice self-affirmation in the same context, your brain will strengthen those circuits instead. With time, positivity will become a norm to you, not because your life has changed all of a sudden, but because you've been reinforcing the neural pathways of hope and resilience.

Also like neuroplasticity, Hebb's law, as affirmed by modern researchers, establishes that our brains are shaped by experience. The only difference is that Hebb's law explains how it happens, while neuroplasticity shows what happens. However, examining both concepts together helps to understand that the brain is flexible and deeply responds to repetition.

Therefore, whether you realize it or not, your repeated actions and thoughts are training your brain. The habits you've formed over time aren't necessarily a product of your personality, according to Hebb's law, they're products of repeated actions being reinforced by neurons. As it stands, every choice you make is either strengthening an old pattern or building a new one. If you realize that yours tilt towards the negative, you should be cautious. If it's towards a positive habit, it's an encouragement.

However, even if harmful habits have been deeply ingrained, be encouraged because you can create new neuron connections to form healthier habits. This requires intentional repetition and practice, however, it's possible. You need to realize that even the smallest actions you do daily matters in your habit formation.

For instance, drinking a cup of water instead of a soda can be the foundation for a new habit. Spending a few minutes to read instead of scrolling on your phone is another example. Also, pausing to breathe before reacting is another powerful action that can become habitual. You just have to repeat them long enough to reshape your brain's pathways. What begins as a single decision, when repeated, has the power to reshape the architecture of the brain itself.

The "Use It or Lose It" Principle

When we were looking at the concept of neuroplasticity together, I mentioned there that it's like building muscles. What happens when you don't regularly exercise your muscles? They'll grow weak, right? Similarly, your brain's neural pathways will become stronger with regular use. They tend to weaken when they're not being used.

This principle is built around brain usage or engagement. It implies that the neurons we regularly activate are kept alive and strengthened. Those you leave unused will automatically fade away slowly. That's to tell you that your brain doesn't waste energy on preserving neuron connections that are no longer in use.

Let's bring it home. The thoughts you entertain, the skills you practice, the emotions you dwell on the most are creating an imprint on your brain. The more you visit them, the neurons involved are fired together again, and their bonds will be strengthened. However, when you begin to ignore some thoughts, practices, or emotions, their neural pathway will become weaker. With time, they'll cease to exist.

Dear reader, unpracticed thoughts can die off!

Ignored emotions can die off!

These are possible because our brains are built for adaptability. It readily trims off whatever isn't prioritized. It knows what you prioritize by what's repeated.

When you start learning a new language, the words and grammar rules may feel foreign. However, if you don't give in at that initial stage because of the difficulty, with consistent practice, the connections responsible for that activity will grow stronger. With time, your words will begin to flow with ease. The rules will become home to you. Your brain will carry on with the new skill. However, try not to speak the language again, your fluency will fade gradually. Once your brain recognizes that those neural pathways aren't in use again, it begins to prune them to make space for what it considers more relevant to your daily life.

This is the same with habits. If you're given to worrying, you're keeping the pathways of anxiety alive and strong. However, if you repeatedly challenge those thoughts and replace them with more hopeful perspectives, the anxious pathways will begin to grow weak. If you persist in the practice of challenging those thoughts, anxious pathways won't only weaken, they'll also fade away. This should, at large, help you to realize that your brain isn't loyal to fear or peace. Its allegiance is primarily to what you practice regularly, and that's what it keeps alive.

Again, like neuroplasticity and Hebb's Law, this principle is also a double-edged sword. One side serves as a caution against neglecting healthy practices, like gratitude, meditation, or compassion. Neglecting them can lead to their gradual decline. The other side of this principle is an assurance that it's possible to be free from tyrannical harmful patterns. What we need to do is to stop feeding them with attention. In their place, we need to start strengthening new pathways. The brain will adapt. Unused neuron connections will fade. It's a natural gift when unused connections fade. You don't have to prompt the brain to eradicate them, it just prunes them off as long as you no longer service them. This will create space for growth.

Have you met people who memorized an entire textbook for an exam, but struggle to recall a fraction of what they memorized many years later? Perhaps you didn't know why that happened then, but now you know. It's not because their memory failed. They only used that information for a particular event. After the event, they did nothing with that information. Long after that, they didn't revisit the information. The brain automatically prunes that neural pathway to make room for more "currently relevant" ones. That's the brain's way of managing its resources efficiently.

One of the bright sides of this principle is that it clearly shows it's possible for new habits to replace old ones. For instance, if a smoker takes a short walk after a meal instead of lighting a cigarette, the old neuron connections of smoking will begin to weaken, while the new one for walking will begin to grow strong. Over time, they'll begin to lose the urge to smoke after eating. This isn't because they erased their past, they just stopped using the former pathway, hence it began to die off.

Hence, what you choose to repeat over and over becomes your present. What you abandon fades away into your past. That's how new habits are formed and strengthened.

Let me spell this out plainly, the "use it or lose it" principle, like the Hebb's law is also at work in your daily engagements. It's been shaping who you're becoming. Nothing in your brain has a permanent residence. It's you who have to determine what you want to retain and keep alive. Even the most consistent thought or habit now can go into extinction if you stop servicing it.

Hence, this is a call for you to be more intentional. Which pathways do you want to reinforce? Which ones do you want to kill? You'll be able to give right answers to these questions after you've decided on the kind of life you want to live hereon. Your responses should also be in line with your values and beliefs.

Again I ask:

- What kind of life do you desire for yourself?
- Does your desire align with your values?
- Going forward, are these choices healthy for you? Will they enhance your well-being?

Growth Mindset Meets Neuroscience

Let's take a last stretch on our discussion about the dynamic nature of your brain and how you can leverage it for a healthier and fulfilling life. With everything we've discussed so far in this chapter about personal transformation, it's obvious that change doesn't happen to anyone by chance. There's a level of deliberate effort that goes into doing the right things to power a healthier lifestyle. In the same breath, growth falls under this same category; it doesn't happen accidentally.

What's the element in the brain that powers growth? Carol Dweck, a psychologist, calls it *mindset*. Everyone has the capacity to become great, but not everyone will become great. Do you know why? Our mindset is the separator. Your mindset can either limit you or propel you forward, it all depends on what you believe. If you think you can't accomplish a thing, truly, you won't. It's what you believe that becomes your reality.

Basically, your mindset talks about the way you perceive yourself and the world around you, and according to Fran (2022), how we see ourselves and our abilities has significant effects on our output daily. When this concept was discussed within the business world, Cote (2022) made reference to a Harvard Business School professor, William Salman, reiterating his query-filled statement:

"Do you have to be young, or technical, or a college dropout, or risk-seeking to become an entrepreneur? I don't think so. Every person can find opportunities, attract necessary resources, and build teams to bring successful products and services to customers." Yes! Everyone can! However, why's everyone not doing this? Mindset!

According to Carol Dweck, the difference between believing that your abilities are fixed and that they can be developed is rooted in your mindset. A growth mindset believes that you've not seen your all yet, your abilities can still be developed. A fixed mindset, however, settles where they are and accept it as their ultimate height.

The shift in your perspective, from fixed to growth mindset, isn't trivial. It courses through everything else, from how you learn, how you handle challenges, how you bounce back from failure, to how you handle your process of becoming. This shift is possible, and the field of neuroscience is also backing this up with biological evidence based on the fact that the brain is designed to adapt, hence, you're capable of change.

Let's revisit the science of neuroplasticity, again. As established earlier, neuroplasticity shows that our brain isn't rigid. It's flexible and adaptable. It's not some finished element that you inherited genetically. Rather, it's a living entity that constantly reshapes itself in response to experiences, learning, and intention.

In the words of Donald Hebb, neurons fire when you try something new. These neuron connections bond even stronger when the activity is being repeated. Hence, a neural pathway that wasn't active before will become a highway through practice. That's proof of the possibility of a growth mindset. In essence, anything you choose to focus on and do persistently through practice not only enhances what you can do, it also changes you at the level of your brain's wiring.

Imagine a child struggling with mathematics. If he has a fixed mindset, his conclusion about his struggle would be, "Well, I'm not a math person." That belief will be his limit. That could make the child lose interest in the subject entirely, hence, leading to disengagement with the subject. Once this happens, the brain will stop investing energy in that pathway. According to the principle of "Use it or Lose it" that connection will weaken and with time, fade away.

If the same child with the same struggle but with a different mindset faces the issue, the outcome will be different. With a growth mindset, the child won't see their struggle as failure, but a signal that their brain is at work. Instead of giving in, they'll stay at it and keep practicing repeatedly. As they make clumsy efforts, make mistakes repeatedly, and review their work again and again, they're giving their brain enough information and time to strengthen the new pathway. Every attempt to get better is transforming the once unfamiliar pathway into a more familiar one.

In neuroscience, it's believed that when we're faced with frustration, it's not a sign that we've hit a wall. It's actually the sound of neurons firing together. New connections are being constructed. Learning is taking place.

Taking a cue from that child's struggle, resilience isn't a vague trait. It's a practice that reshapes the brain. When you persist through a difficult moment, you're strengthening your resolve, but you're also rewriting your mental code. Through your resilience, your brain is learning to hold still in discomfort, search for solutions, and bounce back quickly in the face of unexpected challenges.

In essence, the brain isn't wasting its energy. It's creating and strengthening neural connections. Hence, none of the effort put into learning a thing is wasted; they're all deposits to help your brain build a new pattern.

Adopting a growth mindset facilitates resilience and perseverance. That's the framework the brain needs to build new and stronger neural pathways. When you try to go through new terrains, it's a training ground for your brain. With repetition, you'll become fluent. Mistakes in themselves aren't bad, however, our perceptions about them matter. A growth mindset sees mistakes as a pathway to mastery; that's all the brain needs to keep creating. Scientifically, your brain isn't trying to cope with the challenge, it's rather expanding because of it. In essence, your brain doesn't suffer because of mistakes, it suffers because of your perception and approach to them.

This blend of psychology and biology also reframes failure. In a fixed mindset, failure is final. It is the proof that one has reached their limit. In a growth mindset, supported by neuroscience, failure is data. It is feedback that guides the brain toward a stronger, more resilient network. What looks like defeat from the outside is often the very moment of rewiring on the inside. This is why people who adopt a growth mindset are not deterred by early setbacks. They understand that the brain grows through resistance. Muscles develop when they are pushed. The brain does too.

Your mindset is what you tell yourself through your thoughts. This in itself can shape your brain. Practicing self-criticism will strengthen the neuron connections to grow stronger. Rehearsing discouragement will make the connections become automatic. Conversely, when you cultivate hope, persistence, and positivity, they'll also become stronger. Your brain isn't biased. It simply responds to the ones you focus on more. With a growth mindset, however, you'll be supplying it with material for your transformation.

Chapter Summary

- Your brain is dynamic and powerful. It operates with a system of intentional repetition. Hence, whatever you feed it repeatedly becomes its default response pattern. If you repeatedly feed it with positivity in the face of challenges, it'll become its default response. If you feed it with negativity, it'll become its response pattern.
- You can leverage the fact that your brain isn't biased. It responds to your repeated actions. In essence, your little efforts towards change daily are powerful enough to

transform your whole life experience. Keep at it and it'll become your default pattern.
- Growth doesn't happen by chance, it starts with a mindset. A fixed mindset limits, while a growth mindset propels forward. With a growth mindset, you can persevere through difficult moments till you resolve them. As you do, your brain is learning and creating a new pathway.

11
Why You're Addicted to Your Stories

> Let your story go. Allow yourself to be present with who you are right now.
> – **Russ Kyle**

In 2018, the world's attention was drawn to the mainland of Thailand, where twelve boys from the Wild Boars soccer team and their coach, were trapped in the Tham Luang Cave in Chiang Rai due to a heavy rain that flooded the passageways. For several weeks, the world watched as a diverse attempt to rescue them unfolded. However, it's not the rescue attempt that's most fascinating, it's the narrative that ensured the group's survival.

The boys on the team were between the ages of 11 and 16. How could they have survived such a life-threatening experience? We learned that their strength during that challenge was drawn from their cultural and spiritual beliefs. They had been taught the skill of meditation. One of the core lessons they learned along with that skill was that meditation doesn't just help them calm, it was a technique that helped them perceive suffering as temporary and survival as a mental and physical challenge they must confront. That became the narrative that ensured their survival.

Narratives are powerful. They shape our belief system, and ultimately our thoughts and actions. The memories of your past experience are a form of narrative that could still be influencing your present experiences. This means that to change your experiences, change the narrative.

While some narratives can be so unforgivable and rigid, they're not impossible. Nothing in your brain is cast in stone. They can be rewritten. It's a fact that I'll show you how to leverage in this chapter.

Identity Loops

The first thing that comes to mind when a lot of people hear identity is personality traits. You may picture someone who's shy and never speaks up in a room or someone who's always lively and always has something to say. These descriptions are almost like broad labels, permanent markers that we accept to be true about us. However, let's pause and think about that for a moment. Are our behavioral patterns the same as our identity? Oh, how often we mix them up. We often believe that our behavioral patterns are descriptions of who we are.

However, here's the catch: behavior isn't fixed. It's fluid. It can change with circumstances, seasons of life, and even with the stories you repeat to yourself. That implies that if behavior is changeable, then identity, the version you hold on to in your mind, may not be fixed as you believe it. This is one of the reasons it's important to question the conclusions you've made about yourself.

What if you aren't the shy person you thought you are? What if you're not actually bad at the skill you've always thought you're bad at? However, right now, you're stuck inside that story which reinforces your thoughts and behavioral patterns. So, it's even difficult to believe otherwise.

That story itself is what birthed the idea of an identity loop. An identity loop is something like a mental merry-go-round ride, where you remain in a cycle of repetitive thought and behavioral pattern. Those patterns strengthen what you believe about yourself. This cycle started the moment you began to accept a specific belief about yourself. That belief began shaping your actions. Then your actions also started showing proofs that validate that belief. Then that proof circles back into your identity, which even makes you believe your belief the more. The cycle keeps spinning on and on, until it's no longer a loop to you, but your identity.

For someone who believes that they're not good at public speaking, they'll always feel nervous whenever an opportunity to speak comes up. That belief could make them decline the opportunity. If they eventually force themselves to speak after much persuasion, they'll underperform. After their poor performance, they'll take it as proof that they were never meant for the spotlight. Hence, that belief becomes stronger.

What they don't see is a loop. To them, it's their truth—the truth about who they are. Unknown to them, they've been living in an identity loop.

Identity loops are often disguised as the truth. However, in fact, their stories are built into repeated patterns. The more you retell the story, the more believable it becomes. Repeated thoughts, solidified by repeated behaviors, and reinforced by repeated evidence are the forces behind an identity loop.

This should force you to pause and question what you've believed about yourself all the while.

- Are you who you believe you are?
- Are you caught in an identity loop?

For instance, let's say you've always told yourself, "I'm not creative," (you can put whatever you've been telling yourself.) is that the truth about you or just a repeated story you decided was true after a failed project from years back? Are you truly a shy person or it became true because you avoided certain situations, which became proof of your shyness?

Identity loops have something in common with trauma loops which we discussed in a previous chapter. In a trauma loop, people remain stuck in a moment long after the event happened. They replay that moment in their mind, especially when they're triggered. It influences their behavior and emotions. It's the same with identity loops. Something that happened in the past becomes the standard for defining yourself. Just like trauma loops, identity loops aren't easy to identify because they're subtle, yet powerful. Sometimes, people keep going in that mental cycle without realizing it.

Identity loops started with an event, a narrative, that became a thought pattern. To break the loop, the narrative has to change. What you thought was true about yourself was learned from an experience. It can be unlearned. This still ties back to the science of neuroplasticity. With new experiences, new insights, and new thought patterns, you can change the narrative, and rewire what has been circling in your brain as your truth.

The first step is to challenge that narrative. It'll disrupt that automatic cycle. With that, you'll begin to filter the truth from falsehood, because that loop is actually a lie masquerading as truth.

So, in the instance of someone who thinks they suck at public speaking, challenging that belief can look like this:

What if I'm not actually terrible at this? What if I've just been telling myself I'm terrible?

This question opens them up for a change. Next to this, if they can start practicing small talks, and try to speak up in small meetings and they succeed, they'll begin to create new evidence that usurps that identity loop beliefs. Slowly, the narrative begins to shift. If they persist, that loop will rewire itself. A new identity will begin to emerge—a confident speaker. The more they repeat the new identity, the stronger it becomes.

Another tool for breaking identity loops is self-awareness. The reason you believed that narrative in the first place was because you're not aware of who you are. Without that awareness, you'll keep rehearsing identity loops without questioning them. Self-awareness gives you the ground to query narratives. Just one question, like "Is that who I am truly?" can crack open the identity loop mask, and open up a possibility for change.

What identity loops would you like to crack open?

Emotional Familiarity Bias

Have you seen people who keep returning to the same kind of relationships, habits, or thought patterns, even though those patterns cause them pain? Such experiences make it look like the brain has a comfort zone, a place it feels at home and accustomed to. It's not just about routines or environments, but also emotions. Hence, just as the brain gets familiar with routines and environments, it can get familiar with emotions, too.

The brain's emotional familiarity bias is when the brain has the tendency to gravitate toward an emotion it already knows. Whether the emotion is negative or helpful, it doesn't distinguish that. As long as it's familiar with the emotion, it goes towards it. To the brain, familiar feels safe while the unknown feels threatening. Sadly, what feels safe could be harmful and keep one stuck.

This familiarity bias is one of the explanations for someone who continuously returns to a partner who doesn't give them attention or maltreat them. There's no disputing the fact that they want love and deep connection, however, since their brain has learned to associate emotional distance to familiarity, they stay put in the relationship. Their brain may sound an alarm when someone who's emotionally present comes around them. It's not because it's wrong, but because it feels alien. This means that when it looks like people are self-destructing, it's actually emotional familiarity bias in play.

In Hebb's law, we learned about neurons firing and wiring together, right? One of the reasons the brain invests its energy on active neurons is because it loves to conserve its energy and it loves shortcuts. To the brain, familiar emotions require less processing since the neural pathways have been strengthened over time. That's conserving enough for the brain. It doesn't have to start seeking new pathways to respond to the same issue.

So, if sadness, anxiety, or frustration have been repeatedly experienced, they become neural pathways that are deeply strengthened. The brain tends to existing patterns when new circumstances emerge. Since they've been wired in, it automatically falls back to them.

Guess what the problem is with the familiar? It may not always serve our growth, especially when it's negative. Familiar anger will cloud us from seeing reasons for peace. Familiar fear will hinder us from taking on new opportunities. Familiar shame will keep us locked and bar us from expanding. Emotional familiarity bias can be a prison house that limits a person's endless possibilities. It can keep you running in circles while you keep reliving the same script year in year out. Wondering why it's difficult for you to break out or experience change? Don't look too far. This could just be why.

Joseph LeDoux research in affective neuroscience is one of the works that supports this concept. His work shows that emotional learning often takes place in that part of the brain called amygdala. Learning takes place there real quickly, and it's usually sticky too. Once that part of the brain learns to associate an emotion to a situation, it's usually difficult to unlearn it. This explains why responses like fear or shame often outlasts the event that caused them. It's because as soon as that event happens, the brain treats it as the default response. Change can only happen when that familiarity is interrupted. Else, the familiar will look like the default truth, when they're just a product of repetition.

Why does a person who has made lots of effort to heal from anger find themselves snapping when they're stressed? Their brain associates anger with stress. How about someone who has committed themselves to building a strong and healthy relationship starts feeling attracted to someone who shows similar unhealthy traits as their former partner? It's not because they love to suffer, however, their brain feels it's normal and safe because it's familiar. In essence, like a magnetic force, the brain always gets attracted to the familiar.

However, what feels familiar to the brain now is because it was repeated. The familiar can be broken. The familiar doesn't have to define you. Since the brain itself isn't rigid, new, healthier familiar emotional codes can be rewritten into it. Identifying the codes that need to be broken and replacing them is the first place to start. Don't worry, the new might feel threatening initially, the brain will adapt, it always does. You only have to persist.

Noticing

Self-awareness interrupts the automatic cycle. When you find yourself in an old emotional loop, pause and ask: "Is this truly what I feel, or is it just what I am used to feeling?" This question alone can create space between the emotion and the action. With space comes choice.

Lean into discomfort when it signals growth

If warmth, calm, or acceptance feel uncomfortable, that discomfort may not be a sign of danger but a sign that your brain is stretching. New emotions require practice the same way new skills do. With time, the brain lays down new pathways, and the unfamiliar becomes familiar.

It's also important to remember that breaking emotional familiarity bias isn't about rejecting your past or judging yourself for repeating patterns. It's about gently retraining the brain. Think of it like moving into a new house. At first, you may still drive toward your old address out of habit, but eventually, your brain rewires itself to take you to the new place automatically. The more you practice, the more your emotional GPS updates itself.

Neural Inertia

One fact I've stressed about the brain is its flexibility and adaptability. However, I haven't talked about its tendency to resist change. The brain resisting change can be so frustrating. This tendency is known as *neural inertia*. Even if the change is positive, the brain won't easily bulge, afterall, it's not sentimental.

Let's compare neural inertia to a moving train. Once it picks up speed, and keeps moving on its track, stopping it or switching its direction will require immense energy. That's how it is with the brain.

If you're not used to waking before dawn, you'll struggle with sleepiness when you start it. It's not just sleepiness you're fighting, you're fighting your brain, too. Don't just expect it to adapt easily. Before the new sleeping pattern, it has an established rhythm of rest. To interrupt that will take time and effort. The same thing goes for thoughts, emotional, and behavioral patterns. It will take a lot of effort to get the brain out of its comfortable pattern.

Ever wonder why people love to stick with what they know even though they desire to try something different? Neural inertia is one factor that resists the new. Even if someone desperately desires to leave a job that saps life out of them, their brain will cling to the routine, regardless of the misery. It's not because the news is bad. It's just that it's difficult for it to abandon the old and adapt to a new one.

Even when you want to break the habit of procrastination, you'll realize that when you're about to act, inertia steps in and you're unable to do what you planned to do when you ought to do it. It just loves to stay within its familiar comfort zone. Don't get this wrong, neural inertia isn't that the brain is lazy. It's just its way of conserving its energy. It resists abrupt shifts.

Now you know why it takes a lot of effort to start something new and continue it. After your first day at the gym, it wasn't just your body that doesn't want to get up the next day, your brain is also resisting the change. Getting up early isn't an established pathway, so it'll revolt. That's why change looks prettier on paper than it does in reality.

So you see, wanting to change isn't enough. Your brain needs some persuasion through consistent practice to establish a new pathway. It needs to be convinced that the new pathway is worth the effort. Till it's convinced, it'll try to revert to the old one once and again because it feels familiar, not better.

Do you know why a big opportunity to change your economic status feels like a risk you don't want to take? Your brain has gotten comfortable with surviving, hence a breakthrough risky, and it kicks against it through doubts and fear. To the brain, it's only trying to protect you. Sadly, its protection antagonizes your progress at that moment.

Psychologists sometimes describe neural inertia as the "status quo bias." People prefer to stay with the familiar option, even if it's lesser in quality, because the effort of change feels heavier than the cost of staying the same. The brain is designed to stick until it's retrained to shift.

Start small

Although the very process of retraining the brain can be hard because of inertia, it's not impossible. The brain can be retrained through intentional action. Small, repeated shifts teach the brain that change is survivable, even beneficial. For example, if you're trying to build a new habit like exercising, the brain will initially resist because it prefers rest. However, if you consistently practice short bursts, like 10 minutes a day, the brain begins to ease its resistance. With time, the new routine will become familiar, and inertia shifts in your favour.

Starting small is often more effective than aiming for radical overnight transformation. Neural inertia responds better to gradual rewiring. It's like turning a massive ship. A slight shift in the wheel, if sustained long enough, changes the entire course.

Reframing

Reframe change as continuity instead of disruption. The brain resists abrupt breaks, but it accepts adjustments that feel like natural progressions. So instead of telling yourself, "I have to become a completely different person," it's often better to frame it as, "I'm building on what I already have." This way, you work with inertia rather than against it.

Neural inertia is human, it's not a sign of weakness. However, that resistance isn't the end of the narrative. With patience, repetition, and a willingness to start small, you can shift your brain's momentum. Growth is just around the corner.

Don't judge yourself if you feel stuck. Struggling to change may not just be because you lack willpower, your brain is a factor you've been struggling against all the while without knowing.

Breaking Narrative Addiction Through Language Shifts

Just in case you don't know, we all live inside a narrative. Those narratives are what defines who we are, what we deserve, what we're capable of doing. These stories aren't just abstract ideas, they're the framework our brain uses to interpret reality. The more we repeat them, they become stronger and define our identity, which in turn drives our behavioral patterns.

The problem here is that not all those stories we live by were consciously chosen. We inherited some, some were absorbed, while some others were responses to some past pains. Since the brain is a pattern-seeking organ, it holds on to the familiar scripts and rehearses them until they become second nature. That's what is called narrative addiction.

Let's say you grew up hearing "You're not smart enough," it's quite easy to internalize it and let it play in your mind whenever you face a challenge. If you've experienced people leaving you on different occasions, every other relationship will be seen through the lens of abandonment-tendency. Just like in other previously neural related issues, narrative addiction is powerful because the brain feels safer with familiar stories than the possibility of rewriting it.

Language shifts

This addiction can be broken. According to neuroscience studies, using language shifts as a tool can be revolutionary in changing narratives. The words you use, both in your inner dialogue and outer communication, aren't just descriptive. They're also formative. Every word carries the power to rewire your thought patterns because language and cognition are deeply intertwined. The brain doesn't just process words; it builds worlds out of them.

Check out these two statements:

I'm terrible at this

And

I'm learning how to do this.

There's a whole world of difference between the two and it can shape your perception and action. The first statement is locked on a fixed identity loop, while the second opens up potential for growth. The circumstances may be the same, however, your language frames the struggle differently. While one creates a wall, the other creates a door. When you start to consistently choose door-creating language, it will reshape your brain's default pathways.

There are two exercises that are valid in reshaping your narrative here:

- Affirmations
- Reframing exercises

These aren't just motivational fluffs. They're practical tools for interrupting narrative addiction. Change the words you use to describe yourself and your world, your brain's neural pathways will change because as you speak, you're literally sending new instructions to your neural circuits. Your brain will begin to associate different emotions and possibilities with the same experiences. If you sustain this shift, it'll break the monopoly of the old story.

However, don't expect this to happen overnight. Narrative addiction has taken deep root, especially those you've rehearsed for years. However, through consistency, you can break the old. That's what's called *long-term potentiation.*

Every time you choose a new phrase, you're activating a different neural pathway. Initially, it might feel awkward or untrue, but accept it as your truth and keep practicing it, your brain will start to favour the new route over the old one.

Your brain listens to what you say about yourself. Every "I am" statement creates a neural pathway.

I am anxious.

I am unlucky.

I am not creative.

I am a failure.

I am not good at anything.

I am a nobody.

Harmless, yeah? However, over time, they associate identity with limitations.

Changing your language isn't about denial, it's more about choosing words that give room for growth. Saying, "I am learning to be calm," or, "I am exploring creativity," doesn't ignore your ongoing struggles. It just reframes them in a way that aligns with neuroplasticity, the brain's ability to change.

Be aware of cultural and inherited scripts

Most people are living out narratives that began before them. Families, communities, and societies often pass down phrases that bear great weight. Something like:

"Men don't cry."

"Women must endure."

"This is just how life is."

Those phrases only seem true because we grew up hearing them. Why shouldn't men cry? Is it because the glands are dead? Why must women endure when they can voice out their pains? Why does life have to be this way? Can't it be better?

To break these narratives will require more than an individual effort, it may require an entire community changing its vocabulary. You may not be able to create such change, but surrounding yourself with people who use hopeful languages is like immersing your brain in a new dialect. As you continue in that community, you'll pick up the accent of possibility.

Narrative addiction rides on emotional charge. Those stories you repeat aren't random, they're tied to strong feelings. When you say "I always mess things up," it sticks because it bears the sting of your past failures. You'll need more than mechanical words to break its strength. You have to engage your emotions, too.

Here are some practices that can help you:

- Journaling
- Guided imagery

- Reflective meditation

They all connect language with emotion and allow your new narrative to take a deeper root.

Unlearning Without Disowning

Alvin Toffler is renowned for saying the literate of the twenty-first century isn't just one who can read and write, but one who can learn, unlearn, and relearn. More than ever, that statement is proving true. However, this isn't just about intellectual prowess, it's our well-being. First, unlearning junk that doesn't support our wholeness is crucial.

However, unlearning can sound threatening at first. Contrary to what many people think, unlearning isn't erasing who you are or rejecting everything you've ever known. You're not even disowning your past when you're unlearning. During unlearning, you're creating space to update your patterns of thought, behavior, and belief.

Unlearning is a way of freeing yourself from being bound by those old scripts because they no longer serve you. What you're doing is sorting through what has been stored, letting go of what weighs you down, while you're also keeping what still serves you. Also, you're repurposing what can be transformed.

Recent studies in neuroscience shows why this is so necessary. Our brain is programmed to retain habits and assumptions because of its preference for efficiency. Once it's able to establish the neural pathways, it conserves its energy by reusing them. This explains why certain childhood or formative years beliefs and behaviors continue to shape how we react as adults.

To unlearn, we don't need to uproot the former data, the principles we've learned so far in this book teaches that all we just need to do is to stop using the old neural pathway. It will become weak and eventually fade away as we strengthen new ones. Hence, unlearning isn't deleting the past, it's rewiring the present.

Many people think that they must reject everything from their past to grow. That's not true because things like that often lead to shame or denial, not healing. You don't need to resent your upbringing; you don't have to deny its influence over you either. Instead, acknowledge it, recognize how it once helped you cope, and choose to practice a new language of emotional awareness.

So, while unlearning, you don't have to disown. Honor the role your past played in shaping you as you give yourself the permission to evolve beyond it. Again, remember that disowning often manifests as denial. You might say something like, "That never mattered," when in truth it did matter. However, denial often drives the pain underground, it doesn't heal it. When it goes underground, it continues to influence you in subtle, hidden ways.

There's something called *prediction error* in neuroscience. It's when the brain updates its models when reality contradicts old expectations. That's how unlearning works. Whenever you act against a limiting belief and experience a different outcome, your brain registers a prediction error. As you keep repeating it and the outcome remains the same, the repeated mismatch forces the brain to update. The old narrative will weaken, while the new one becomes stronger and available. However, you can't change what you refuse to face, that's why this update requires honesty about the past narrative.

With reframing, you can begin to see your past differently, instead of denying it. Hence, rather than seeing your past as a series of mistakes, you can reinterpret it as your training material. The difficult period you experienced might have wired you to be hypervigilant, but you can redirect it into discernment and leadership. Self-doubt that once protected you from criticism can be redirected to fuel humility which makes you teachable. Your experience isn't wasted. There is some deep wisdom in your pain, too.

Experiencing growth doesn't mean you have to pretend your trauma never happened. Integrating the lessons you learned during that experience is what enlarges your future. Even though the scars remain, they no longer call the shot on how far you can go.

Why Letting Go of Old Stories Feels Like Grief

I know how it feels to decide to let go of old narratives that have shaped you over the years. It often comes with a strange ache. You might expect to feel lighter, unburdened, even liberated, instead, you'll be stung with sadness first. Instead of feeling more like freedom, it's more like grief. That's because it's actually grief.

Those old narratives you're about to let go aren't just memories, they're maps that have helped you survive for as long as you've had them. A child who learned to stay silent in a tense home isn't just merely quiet. They'll learn that silence and invisibility is the best way to stay safe. For someone who only earns praise whenever they do well at something learns to believe that they have to always perform well to be loved.

With those stories, those individuals were able to make sense of their world. So, since it worked for them over time, helping them to survive, their brain stored it as their truth. That's what many of us experienced.

Now that you're an adult, when you attempt to challenge things you learned in your childhood, it feels like you're tearing down something sacred. You're not only questioning beliefs, you're quieting an entire coping strategy that once held your world together. Do you see why you'll feel sad when letting go? When you feel this way, it's not a sign that you're weak. It's recognizing your loss.

Psychologists often refer to this as a secondary loss (Harrington-LaMorie, 2013). When you lose a person, it's not just them you lose, you also lose routines, expectations, and identity roles attached to them. That's how it is with letting go of an old narrative. You're losing the roles, relationships, and identity structures that the narrative shaped. Grieving goes beyond bereavement. It also comprises loss of a central organizing force. That's exactly the purpose old narratives serve, too, no matter how painful.

When you're grieving over losing an old narrative, though it hurts, grief isn't asking you to turn back. It's telling you that change is imminent. That version of you that survived through that narrative is giving way to another narrative.

Oftentimes, when we're letting go, regret is another thing we feel. Regret over lost times and opportunities. However, it's also an indication that meaning-making can turn regret into wisdom. The old narrative, instead of being seen as wasted time, can be viewed as the right training for a different life.

Therapists often encourage people to approach this process as a form of mourning. One helpful model is the *dual process model of grief* developed by Stroebe and Schut in 2016. This model teaches that healthy grieving goes in two directions. Some days you face the loss head-on. You feel the sadness. You acknowledge the void. Other days, focus on restoration, building new habits, and leaning into new meaning. Both movements are important. The same movement is necessary for letting go of old narratives. It doesn't happen on a straight line. You toggle between what you're losing and what you are building.

A profound practice to ease this process is *writing a farewell letter to your old narrative.*

In the letter, thank it for the role it played in your life. Acknowledge how it tried to protect you. Grieve what it cost you. Then release it. Sounds simple, right? This practice will help you engage both emotion and cognition. Those who have practiced it discovered that it lessened shame and made space for compassion.

Ultimately, grief isn't an enemy of growth. It's proof that growth is taking place. On the other side of grief is reinvention. Neural pathways rewire. New stories take shape. Slowly, the new identity stops feeling foreign and begins to feel natural. The grief lessens. Freedom expands.

Hence, though you grief while letting go of old narratives, you're actually gaining the chance to write new ones. Stories that no longer confine but expand. Stories that don't shrink you but allow you to breathe.

Chapter Summary

- Narratives are powerful tools for defining who you are, how you behave, and what you believe. Narratives that are rooted in your past pain may feel like your truth, but they're not the truth because they're products of distorted negative experiences. Hence, you can't keep living with them if you must experience transformation.
- Your brain readily resists new narratives, not because it hates change, but because it's trying to protect you. Any new information that it's not familiar with, it flags it as a threat, even if it's a positive change. That's why rewiring the brain to adapt to new changes has to be done with small consistent actions repeatedly.
- Language is a powerful tool for shaping your identity and your world. Your brain listens to what you say about yourself, and

uses it to create your responses. If you say negative things about yourself, you're limiting yourself because that's what the brain registered. Through reframing and affirmation, you can rewrite your experiences.

12

The Truth About Control

Incredible change happens in your life when you decide to take control of what you do have power over instead of craving control over what you don't.
— Steve Maraboli

Something shocking happened in 2021 during the 2020 Olympics held in Tokyo. Simone Biles, who has carved her name in history books as one of the greatest gymnasts, shocked the world when she withdrew from multiple events. She was at the peak of her career, and many millions of people were expecting her to win gold. However, Biles decided to step back.

Why? She said she had mental health struggles and a loss of spatial awareness during high-risk maneuvers. NBC News reported her saying that she had to withdraw because she wanted to focus on her mental health and not jeopardize her health and well-being.

This decision by a globally-recognized athlete sparked global conversations. People had high expectations of her. However, she also had to take care of herself. She had control over taking care of herself, that's internal, but people's expectations, that's external and there was nothing she could do about that, because people's expectations are transient and can be swayed. Hence, she channeled her energy to what she could control—her well-being.

Not many people would agree with Biles, but she made the best choice for herself. With that she lengthened her days and relevance. If she had continued with that tournament, something disastrous could have ensued. The world would mourn, but they will move on.

Learning to prioritize what really matters and focusing on that is essential to your wholeness. In this case what really matters, and which deserves your attention, is what's within your ambit of control. As we wrap up this journey, we'll pay attention to what you can control and what you can't to help you optimize your strength.

Internal Vs External Locus of Control

Have you ever wondered how some folks tend to take control of their lives, with the belief that they're the shape of their destiny, while there are some other folks who wait for life to happen to them because they believe that they're merely sojourners passing through life, with no control over their destination?

What's the difference between these two groups? It's in something psychologists call the locus of control. It's a simple idea—where do you believe control truly lives? If you think your actions influence your outcomes, that's an internal locus of control. When you feel that life's direction is mostly due to luck, other people, or situations outside your influence, that's an external locus of control.

This isn't just a theory or a label. Your sense of control subtly shapes how you respond to daily challenges. If you've ever thought, "I can improve this situation," you're aligning with an internal control orientation. But if your first thought is, "There's nothing I could do," that tilt toward external control becomes clear.

There's strength and flexibility in believing you're responsive to life rather than at its mercy. A recent survey of over 3,000 Danish adults found that those who believed they can actively improve their mental well-being actually reported better mental health outcomes (Cassata, 2022). It's not magic. It's the brain's wiring. Believing your choices matter, even if it's as small as practicing gratitude or self-care, your brain begins to scan for evidence that you're not just reacting to life, you're shaping it.

And this matters beyond feelings. More internal control is tied to stronger self-control and healthier habits. A large Australian study showed that people with more internal control tend to exercise better self-control, and together, these traits predict better physical and mental health outcomes (Botha & Dahmann, 2024). This means that when you feel capable of influencing life, you're also more likely to follow through on what matters to you.

However, there are times when the circumstances we face are genuinely out of our control. What should we do in those moments? You see, leaning into an external perspective in such moments isn't weakness, it's realistic. No one would blame someone for attributing heartbreak to unfair events in their path. However, the trap is letting that perspective dominate long after the storm passes.

In recent years, researchers have also connected locus of control with emotional resilience. A study carried out on students revealed that both self-monitoring and internal control contributed to increased psychological resilience (Shanava & Gergauli, 2023). In essence, believing you can influence your responses makes you better equipped to handle stress, bounce back from setbacks, and lean into growth.

This idea of resilience has practical implications too. A conceptual analysis focusing on women facing high-risk pregnancies showed that an internal sense of control supported healthier coping, anxiety reduction, and better engagement with care plans. When the future felt unpredictable and fraught, believing they had a voice in their care helped them act, rather than retreat.

Still, internal control isn't always the clear winner. When faced with systemic or unfair situations—like workplace bullying—internal people may feel powerless when they actually lack structural safeguards. In one study of workplace bullying, those with strong internal control felt the most strain when exposed to abuse, while those with external control were less emotionally affected by the same bullying (Reknes et al., 2019). That doesn't mean internal control is weak. It shows that context matters. Believing you can influence outcomes works when you truly can, but it can leave you feeling blamed when you can't.

So how do we work with this? First, noticing your natural orientation helps. Do you tend to ask, "What could I do?" or do you think, "It was just bad luck again"? Neither is shameful, but knowing your bias gives you the chance to flex toward the other side when needed.

Second, language matters. Instead of saying, "There's nothing I can change," try, "What's one small thing I can influence?" That shift doesn't deny reality. It simply acts as a gentle bridge toward possibility.

Third, behaviors build belief as much as thoughts do. When you're doing something within your control, no matter how little, the brain is encouraged to register, "I had a hand in that." With time, your brain will start expecting your input to matter, that's an inward shift in the loci of control.

It is worth repeating this isn't about being blind to injustice. Healthy internal control means recognizing what you can influence and what genuinely lies outside your reach. It's not about blaming yourself for lack of control. It's about choosing where energy is well directed.

In modern psychology, internal locus of control also predicts better mental health. For example, students who internalize control report lower anxiety, better adjustment, and overall emotional stability. Especially in transitions—like university, or starting a new job—that internal lens seems to anchor the mind in growth, not fear.

Overall, this orientation towards control becomes a kind of self-fulfilling prophecy. If you believe your choices matter, you tend to make them matter. Your brain interprets win and loss differently. Effort becomes evidence. Notably, a growing body of work confirms that even in adulthood, brains can shift toward more adaptive wiring when we challenge old patterns.

So if you feel stuck in a story that life just happens to you, know this: the story isn't your identity. It's a habit that can be rewritten, line by line, thought by thought, choice by choice. Every small step toward owning what you can influence rewires the brain to expect more agency. Over time, you're not just hoping life can change—you're showing yourself that it can.

What Real Agency Looks Like Neurologically

Acting with intention and making choices that align with who you want to be is called agency. However, how does this play out in the brain?

Modern neuroscience reveals that agency isn't only a philosophical concept, it's a measurable function of how the brain interprets information, processes past occurrences, and guides future behavior.

There are three things central to agency:

- Awareness
- Choice
- Action

Awareness

It's your ability to recognise what's happening in and around you without immediately defaulting to old patterns.

Choice

How you evaluate different options and select the one that relates to your desired outcome, not just one that seems most familiar.

Action

This is the point where the brain signals the body to move, speak, or respond in a way that expresses intentional living.

Neurologically, this process engages multiple brain regions. Let's begin with the prefrontal cortex. It acts like the brain's executive office, with planning, weighing consequences, and overriding automatic impulses. When you consciously decide to respond calmly to criticism rather than lash out, it's your prefrontal cortex at work. Then there's the basal ganglia. It's often linked with habit formation. It's the part that translates these conscious decisions into repeatable patterns. So, the more you practice deliberate responses, the more they become wired into your brain. It reduces the mental energy required to act with agency.

Neuroscience also reveals that agency thrives when the brain experiences a sense of coherence between intention and action. Studies showed that when people felt in control of their choices, their brains showed higher levels of activity in areas associated with reward and motivation. That means that the brain itself strengthens the experience of agency; it's likely to seek it out again. That's why small acts of decision-making, like choosing a morning routine or setting boundaries with a colleague, can lead into larger patterns of self-directed living.

However, real agency isn't only about decision-making; it's also about recognizing where automatic scripts have been running your life. Some of those scripts are rooted in past experiences, used as survival mechanisms. For instance, if you grew up in an unpredictable household, you might become hyper-vigilant. This state of constant alertness feels like you're in control, but neurologically it's the opposite. It's your amygdala keeping your body alert for threat instead of letting the prefrontal cortex guide intentional action. That's why developing agency often requires shutting down fear-based responses and empowering neural pathways for thoughtful reflection.

Self-talk is one of the tools that can be used to significantly increase activities in neural circuits that are linked to motivation and resilience. This will translate into growth and possibilities.

Agency isn't a static trait; it's a skill that can be developed. Whenever you consciously override an old habit, query a limiting belief, or choose a response that reflects your values, you strengthen the neural connections that support agency. The more you practice, the more your brain becomes primed to seek out and seize opportunities for intentional living instead of defaulting to familiar but limiting patterns.

This also explains why lapses in agency are not signs of failure but opportunities for learning. Neurologically, the best way the brain learns is through what's called *error correction*. When you notice you're falling into an old pattern, and you intentionally course-correct, your brain reinforces the new pathway even more strongly. It isn't perfection but repetition that rewires the brain for agency.

It's important to state here that real agency isn't about control in every circumstance. It's recognizing what you can influence and taking ownership of that space. The brain naturally seeks predictability, but agency asks you to step into uncertainty with a mindset to explore.

The Spheres of Influence Model

This is a framework that helps us understand the extent of control and impact an individual truly has over different aspects of life. It takes away the illusion that everything can be controlled and helps one focus attention on the areas that intentional efforts can yield meaningful change. To build agency, you'll need this model because it teaches individuals to channel their energy where it matters most and let go of what's outside their control.

The Spheres of Influence Model divides life into three concentric zones.

- **Control**

This is the sphere of control where you have direct power over your actions, attitudes, habits, and choices.

So, while you may not be able to control an element as the weather, you can control your daily routines, emotional responses, and the mindset you use to approach the condition. When you strengthen your awareness of what you can control, there will be significant reduction in stress, and increase in resilience. (Beck, 2020).

- **Influence**

This talks about things you can't influence but through relationships, persuasion, and consistent behavior, you can impact them. For instance, you might not be able to control every aspect of a group's performance as a team lead, however, through clear communication and supportive leadership, you can shape the team's performance and outputs. Also, parents can't directly influence their child's decisions, however, they can influence their choices by modeling values and creating an environment of trust.

- **Concern**

This pertains to the issues that matter to you deeply but are beyond your direct control. The issues in this category are global events, governmental policies, and societal shifts. Although you may feel powerless in these areas, the model doesn't suggest ignoring them. What you should do instead is align your energy.

Obsessing over things you can't control can lead to emotional exhaustion. However, while acknowledging them and returning focus to the inner spheres preserves mental well-being and effectiveness. In Stephen Covey's *The 7 Habits of Highly Effective People*, this approach is called living proactively, that is channeling focus toward what you can act on rather than reacting to what you can't.

Neurologically, this model aligns with how the brain processes threats and possibilities. When you dwell too much on the sphere of concern, your amygdala, which regulates fear and anxiety, becomes overactive. This can lead to chronic stress and feelings of helplessness.

Conversely, when you focus on the sphere of control, you're engaging your prefrontal cortex, and that's the part of your brain that facilitates decision-making, planning, and self-regulation.

To practice the Spheres of Influence Model, there are three steps involved:

1. **Identification.**

This is where you learn to identify and distinguish between what you can control, what you have influence over, and what you're merely concerned about.

To identify these three, you might need to practice honest reflection and journaling because daily frustrations tend to blur these lines.

2. **Realignment.**

Once you've been able to identify, your energy should, hence, be redirected to actions within the sphere of your influence and control. This will allow your mental and emotional resources to be used productively.

3. **Reinforcement**

Repeated and consistent practice of this model will rewire the neural pathways so that your brain will naturally default to problem-solving instead of rumination.

This model can also deeply influence your interpersonal relationships. Conflicts often arise when the parties involved attempt to control each other rather than influence them positively. This could happen between parents and their child, leaders and followers, boss and workers. Recognizing the difference between the levels of this model will prevent emotional overextension and foster healthier connections.

Also, this model strengthens the importance of boundaries. By clarifying what's outside your personal control, you can practice emotional detachment without apathy. You're not becoming indifferent to societal or global issues, however, you're identifying the fact that your greatest contribution begins with what you can control within your immediate environment.

It's just like saying that a community leader should single-handedly end poverty. They can't. However, they can start initiatives within their neighborhood. They can also influence others to join them, and even start advocating for policy changes through collective effort. These actions will ripple outward and extend influence into spheres that initially seemed unreachable.

Control Addiction

Control addiction isn't wanting things to be done well. It's about needing things to be done in a way that silences an inner sense of fear and unease. On the surface, perfectionism and micromanagement appear like traits that are of highly organized and disciplined individuals. People celebrate them in workplaces as signs of commitment and high standards. However, beneath the surface lies a less apparent truth because those behavioral patterns are often fuelled by anxiety, not confidence.

Most times, we pay attention to what anxiety feels like in our body, but in the brain, it's a heightened sense of threat. When your amygdala becomes hyperactive, it's because you're feeling vulnerable. This overactivation doesn't just warn of real dangers, it also triggers false alarms. It convinces the mind that things will go wrong unless every detail is tightly controlled. That's why anxiety often hides behind perfectionism. Focusing on making everything flawless, the mind tries to quiet the fear of failure. That's how Micromanagement works, too.

It offers a temporary sense of security by keeping everything under close supervision.

Studies have shown that perfectionism has more to do with emotional unease than with excellence. Perfectionists often set unrealistically high standards, that leaves them in a constant state of pressure and dissatisfaction. So, instead of feeling fulfilled by achievement, they feel voidness. They remain tense and hyper-vigilant, fearing that any small mistake will confirm their worst fears.

This emotional pressure feeds into what can be called control addiction. It's an overreliance on control as a coping mechanism. This cycle is a loop between anxiety and hypervigilance. The more anxious a person feels, the more they attempt to control. Yet, the more they control, the more they reinforce their anxiety because the brain learns that safety only comes through extreme effort and monitoring.

The workplace is one area where this is clearly seen. Leaders who struggle with control addiction often mask it as a commitment to quality. They review every task, correct every mistake, and insist on rigid adherence to their way of doing things. At first, this seems like high performance. When a team is led by a micromanaging leader, they'll experience lower morale, creativity, and engagement. The team members will feel stifled, and innovation will slow down because the leader's anxiety-driven need for control won't allow space for mistakes or exploration.

From a neurological standpoint, the brain doesn't relax under these conditions. The prefrontal cortex struggles to override the constant stress signals from the amygdala. Instead of focusing on big-picture problem-solving, the brain stays locked in threat response mode, reinforcing the belief that control is necessary at all times. Over time, this creates mental fatigue and heightens the risk of burnout.

However, breaking free from control addiction doesn't mean abandoning standards or letting go of responsibility. It means recognizing the difference between healthy control and compulsive control. Healthy control allows for delegation, flexibility, and learning from mistakes. Compulsive control leaves no room for error because the mind interprets imperfection as danger. Acceptance and self-compassion in overcoming perfectionism can help retrain the brain to see mistakes as opportunities rather than threats.

The first challenge you'll confront while letting go of control is feeling deeply uncomfortable. Letting go for a perfectionist will require tolerating uncertainty and trust that not everything must be perfectly managed to turn out well. Still this discomfort is part of rewiring the brain. Through learning to pause when the urge to over-control arises and by gradually allowing space for imperfection, the brain forms new patterns. It starts to associate safety not with control but with adaptability and resilience.

This shift has ripple effects beyond individual wellbeing. In workplaces, it fosters environments where trust and creativity flourish. In personal life, it allows relationships to feel less strained and more collaborative. Most importantly, it helps reduce anxiety at its root rather than reinforcing it through relentless perfectionism and micromanagement.

Therefore, control addiction isn't just a behavioral issue. It's a neurological loop driven by emotional discomfort. Understanding this connection helps us see that true agency is not about controlling everything. It's about recognizing what needs control and what needs trust, and choosing wisely.

Reclaiming Agency

Describing agency earlier, we called it the centre of decision-making and purposeful action. It's a measurable function with three core job descriptions: awareness, choice, action. These three core functions to anyone who desires to be in control of their lives instead of being driven by external factors.

Hence, when we talk about reclaiming agency, it's about assuming the driver's seat of your life, especially when old narratives, conditioned responses, and external influences have been shaping your choices for years. This isn't about forcing control over every situation; it's not about pretending that life will always bend to your will either. Rather, it's coming into an awareness of the small but powerful space between what happens and how you respond, then making intentional choices in that moment. That space is where your power lives, and the more you practice using it, the stronger it becomes.

Agency is present in every small daily decision. Even though you may not be able to control what someone says to you, you can control how you interpret them and how you let them define your mood. You don't have power over the challenges life throws at you, but you can choose how you interpret them. These shifts might seem simple, however, they're deeply transformative. With time, those actions will rewire your brain. They'll recreate new neural pathways that support conscious responses instead of automatic reactions steeped in fear or self-doubt.

This process of reclaiming agency is also called emotional work. When you've lived for years under stories of failure, inadequacy, or rejection, stepping into a new sense of power can feel exciting and uncomfortable all at once. Fear often rises, not because you are doing something wrong, but because your brain is adjusting to a new way of living. Old stories offer a strange sense of comfort, even when they keep you stuck. Reclaiming agency challenges those familiar patterns and invites you to embrace growth, which is often unknown territory.

How to Reclaim Agency

Change your language

Words don't just describe your reality; they shape it. When you say "I can't handle this," you're telling your brain to shut down, while saying, "I'm learning to handle this" keeps you open to possibility. The shift may feel small, but it plants seeds of resilience and curiosity. Each time you choose empowering words, you remind yourself that you are capable of growth and change.

Reconnect with your values

When life feels out of control, it's often because you've drifted away from what matters most and started living according to someone else's expectations. Values act as anchors in uncertain times. They help you make choices that align with who you are becoming, rather than who you were taught to be. When decisions flow from your core values, you feel a greater sense of clarity and calm because your actions are rooted in meaning.

Self-compassion

Reclaiming agency isn't something that happens from a one-time event where everything suddenly shifts. It's a daily practice. Sometimes you'll slip back into old patterns. That's not failure; it's feedback. Beating yourself up only reinforces the very stories you're trying to release.

Instead, celebrate small wins. Notice the moments when you paused instead of reacting or when you made a choice that reflected your true values. These moments may seem minor, but they carry weight. They build evidence that you can show up differently, and with each choice, your confidence grows.

Learn where your influence ends

Agency is not about trying to control outcomes that are beyond your reach. It's about owning what you can do while letting go of what you can't. This balance keeps you from slipping into frustration or self-blame when things don't go as planned. It allows you to invest your energy wisely into actions, mindsets, and habits that create genuine progress, rather than wasting it on what was never yours to control.

The work of reclaiming agency also reshapes how you view challenges. Instead of seeing them as proof that life is against you, you begin to see them as opportunities to practice choice. Even when situations are hard, you can choose how you show up. You can choose to ask for help, to learn something new, or to approach the moment with courage instead of fear. These choices may not change the circumstances overnight, but they change you, and that shift is where transformation begins.

These small, intentional actions build a life that feels more authentic and less driven by default patterns. You start to recognize that your agency was never truly lost; it was only buried under old stories, fears, and learned helplessness. As you reclaim it, you remember who you are. You're that person who's capable of responding with clarity, acting with purpose, and shaping a life that reflects your deepest values.

Reclaiming agency isn't about becoming perfect. It's about presence, awareness. It's recognizing that no matter what has shaped your past, you have the power to shape what comes next. Therefore, each moment is a chance to choose again. Now, you can choose courage, purpose, and growth over the pull of old narratives. When you make this choice over and again, it creates a life of genuine freedom.

Chapter Summary

- In reality, there are things you can control, things you can influence, and things you are concerned about. Distinguishing these three areas in your life, through meditative reflection and journaling, will help you optimize your life and maximize your strength
- Your energy will be better maximized and productive if you channel them towards what you can control first. Focusing on what you can't will sap you of your essence and make you circle back into a deep hole of frustration. Identify what you can control and focus your energy on it.
- Reclaiming agency is crucial to your becoming. Rephrase your words to be more positive, clearly define your values and align your actions with them, then patiently make small meaning choices daily. Ensure your choices align with your values as well. With self-compassion, you'll patiently rewire your brain's neural pathway as you constantly repeat these actions.

CONCLUSION

What an explorative journey into the vast territory of your mind! So many lessons and insights to draw from here. Also, so much rebuilding is taking place here already. While exploring your vast mind, we discovered that your mind can be a noisy neighbour, a fearful storyteller, and a relentless critic. Yet, it's also powerful and capable of extraordinary change. Your mind also happens to be an open battlefield where anyone with the best strategy and tools can control whatever goes on there.

Also, during this journey, we explored how mental clutter, fear-driven instincts, comparison, and worst-case thinking can quietly drain your joy and shape your reality without you even noticing. Then we also established that science isn't an enemy of hope, but a roadmap to freedom.

By exploring neuroscience, we learned that thoughts aren't permanent truths; they're chemical patterns that can be rewired. Belief can shift. Memories can be edited. Emotions can move through you instead of trapping you. This implies that change isn't mystical, it's methodical. It's not reserved for a lucky few, it's rather a series of steps, repeated with intention, until the brain itself begins to rewire its neural pathways to respond to life's matters.

One of the most powerful facts we're able to establish in this book is that you're not your thoughts. You're the observer who can notice, question, and redirect them. When fear hijacks your logic, you can

Conclusion

pause and choose reason. When comparison creeps in, you can step back and remember that your worth was never up for debate. When worst-case scenarios flood your mind, you can refuse to live inside a future that hasn't happened.

The real breakthrough is agency. Understanding that you don't have control over everything that happens to you is truly liberating. You may not control what life brings you, however you can control where your attention goes. You can control which beliefs you feed, and your narratives about yourself. These choices shape everything, from your emotions to your behaviors and the way your brain fires in the next moment.

Hence, true transformation starts with understanding that freedom begins the moment you stop waiting for your mind to behave and start training it to serve you. The 90-second pause, the practice of emotional agility, the rewiring of old patterns, and the courage to let go of old narratives are strategies, as well as lifelines, for change.

After learning so much, taking one step at a time to experience the things you've learned is crucial. Establish your personal routine, it can be a small action you'll be committed to daily. You're registering something in your brain with it no matter how long it takes. Just keep repeating it consistently.

Notice your thoughts without judgment. Catch the moment fear tries to hijack you. Speak to yourself with affirmative words that build, not break you. Keep choosing what you can control and release what you can't.

This isn't about becoming perfect, rather, it's becoming present, intentional, and free. Your brain will resist at first; it's trying to protect you. However, it'll adapt when you persist and it notices the outcome. Every new thought you repeat, every pause you take, every story you rewrite is proof you're not at the mercy of your mind. You're its trainer and guide.

As you prepare to write the next chapters of your experiences, will you let your old patterns and narratives write it for you or will you take the pen?

I'd like your feedback and let me know what narratives you're rewriting. Your story will be an interesting read!

REFERENCE

Al-Mosaiwi, M., & Johnstone, T. (2018). In an absolute state: Elevated use of absolutist words is a marker specific to anxiety, depression, and suicidal ideation. Clinical Psychological Science, 6(4), 529–542. https://doi.org/10.1177/2167702617747074

American Psychiatric Association. (2013). Diagnostic and statistical manual of mental disorders (5th ed.). American Psychiatric Publishing.

Andrews-Hanna, J. R., Reidler, J. S., Sepulcre, J., Poulin, R., & Buckner, R. L. (2010). Functional-anatomic fractionation of the brain's default network. Neuron, 65(4), 550–562. https://doi.org/10.1016/j.neuron.2010.02.005

Anticevic et al. (2012) – "The role of default network deactivation in cognition and disease"

Arnsten, A. F. T. (2009). Stress signalling pathways that impair prefrontal cortex structure and function. Nature Reviews Neuroscience, 10(6), 410-422. https://doi.org/10.1038/nrn2648

Baumeister, R. F., Bratslavsky, E., Finkenauer, C., & Vohs, K. D. (2001). Bad is stronger than good. Review of general psychology, 5(4), 323-370.

Beck, A. T. (1976). Cognitive therapy and emotional disorders. New American Library.

Bedsworth, J. (2022, July 12). *What Is Emotional Agility and How to Practice It*. GoodRx. https://www.goodrx.com/health-topic/mental-health/how-to-practice-emotional-agility

Beins, K. (2022, January 31). *Using Hebb's Law to Our Advantage - Kelly Beins*. Kelly Beins. https://www.kellybeins.com/using-hebbs-law-to-our-advantage/

Berridge, K. C., & Robinson, T. E. (2016). Liking, wanting, and the incentive-sensitization theory of addiction. American Psychologist, 71(8), 670–679. https://doi.org/10.1037/amp0000059

BetterHelp Editorial Team. (2025, February 18). *An Overview Of False Memory & What Causes It | Betterhelp*. Www.betterhelp.com. https://www.betterhelp.com/advice/memory/an-overview-of-false-memory-what-causes-it/

Botha, F., & Dahmann, S. C. (2024). Locus of control, self-control, and health outcomes. *SSM-Population Health*, *25*(1), 101566–101566. https://doi.org/10.1016/j.ssmph.2023.101566

Bradfield, P. (2022, September 28). *The Trauma Loop - WinShape Homes*. WinShape Homes. https://homes.winshape.org/update/the-trauma-loop/

Brunet, A. (2025). *How editing trauma memories with Reconsolidation Therapy^{TM} could change PTSD treatment*. Usc.edu.au; University of the Sunshine Coast. https://www.usc.edu.au/about/unisc-news/news-archive/2025/may/how-editing-trauma-memories-with-reconsolidation-therapy-could-change-ptsd-treatment

Carter, R. (2024, July 15). *Boost Your Success Through Emotion Tagging - Dr. Roddy Carter*. Dr. Roddy Carter. https://roddycarter.com/personal-growth/emotion-tagging/

Cassata , C. (2022, July 30). *Believing You Can Improve Your Mental Well-Being Works*. Verywell well. https://www.verywellmind.com/believing-you-can-improve-your-mental-well-being-helps-5536948

Conclusion

Cherry, K. (2024, May 17). *How neuroplasticity works*. Verywell well. https://www.verywellmind.com/what-is-brain-plasticity-2794886

Clark, L., & Zack, M. (2023). Getting a buzz from likes: Social media and gambling share reward learning mechanisms. Current Opinion in Behavioral Sciences, 50, 101254. https://doi.org/10.1016/j.cobeha.2023.101254

Cote, C. (2022, March 10). *Growth mindset vs. fixed mindset: What's the difference?* Harvard Business School Online. https://online.hbs.edu/blog/post/growth-mindset-vs-fixed-mindset

David, S., & Congleton, C. (2013, November). *Emotional Agility*. Harvard Business Review. https://hbr.org/2013/11/emotional-agility

Davies M. I., & Clark D. M. (2025). Thought suppression produces a rebound effect with analogue post-traumatic intrusions. *Behav Res Ther*, *36*, 571–582. https://www.psy.ox.ac.uk/publications/809406

Dean, M. E. (2022, August 25). *What Is Denial Psychology & How To Address It | Betterhelp*. Www.betterhelp.com. https://www.betterhelp.com/advice/general/what-is-denial-psychology-how-to-address-it/

Draganski, B., Gaser, C., Busch, V., Schuierer, G., Bogdahn, U., & May, A. (2004). Neuroplasticity: changes in grey matter induced by training. Nature, 427(6972), 311–312. https://doi.org/10.1038/427311a

Evans, J. S. B. T. (2008). Dual-processing accounts of reasoning, judgment, and social cognition (review). Annual Review of Psychology.

Fazio, L. K., Brashier, N. M., Payne, B. K., & Marsh, E. J. (2015). Knowledge does not protect against illusory truth. *Journal of Experimental Psychology: General, 144*(5), 993–1002. https://doi.org/10.1037/xge0000098

Finkelstein, S., Whitehead, J., & Campbell, A. (2019). *HOW EMOTIONAL TAGGING CAN PUSH LEADERS TO MAKE BAD DECISIONS* •. Iveybusinessjournal.com. https://iveybusinessjournal.com/publication/how-emotional-tagging-can-push-leaders-to-make-bad-decisions/

Fran. (2022, April 25). *What is a growth mindset and how can you develop one?* FutureLearn. https://www.futurelearn.com/info/blog/general/develop-growth-mindset

Frederick, S. (2005). Cognitive Reflection and Decision Making (CRT). Journal / AEA paper.

Gigerenzer, G., Todd, P. M., & the ABC Research Group. Fast and Frugal Heuristics (adaptive heuristics critique).

Grühn, D., Lumley, M. A., Diehl, M., & Labouvie-Vief, G. (2013). Time-based indicators of emotional complexity: Interrelations and correlates. *Emotion, 13*(2), 226–237. https://doi.org/10.1037/a0030363

Hamilton et al. (2011) – "Default-mode and task-positive network activity in major depressive disorder: implications for adaptive and maladaptive rumination"

Hanson-Baiden, J. (2022, January 10). *The Debate on Repressed Memories.* News-Medical.net. https://www.news-medical.net/health/The-Debate-on-Repressed-Memories.aspx

Harrington-LaMorie, J. (2013, March 21). *Recognizing and Grieving Secondary Losses.* Www.taps.org. https://www.taps.org/articles/19-1/secondaryloss

Conclusion

Hofmann, S. G., Asnaani, A., Vonk, I. J., Sawyer, A. T., & Fang, A. (2022). The Efficacy of Cognitive Behavioral Therapy: A Review of Meta-analyses. Cognitive Therapy and Research, 46(6), 1051–1072. https://doi.org/10.1007/s10608-021-10253-4

Hunt, M. G., Marx, R., Lipson, C., & Young, J. (2018). No more FOMO: Limiting social media decreases loneliness and depression. Journal of Social and Clinical Psychology, 37(10), 751–768. https://doi.org/10.1521/jscp.2018.37.10.751

Hutchinson, J. (2024). *Illusory truth effect | EBSCO*. EBSCO Information Services, Inc. | Www.ebsco.com. https://www.ebsco.com/research-starters/psychology/illusory-truth-effect

Kabat-Zinn, J. (2013). Full catastrophe living: Using the wisdom of your body and mind to face stress, pain, and illness (Revised ed.). Bantam Books.

Kahneman, D., & Tversky, A. (1979). Prospect Theory: An Analysis of Decision under Risk. Econometrica.

Kimble, M., Fleming, K., Bandy, C., Kim, J., & Zambetti, A. (2013). Eye tracking and visual attention to threat in veterans of the Iraq war. Journal of Anxiety Disorders, 24(3), 293–299. https://doi.org/10.1016/j.janxdis.2009.01.006

LeDoux, J. E. (2007). The amygdala. Current Biology, 17(20), R868-R874. https://doi.org/10.1016/j.cub.2007.08.005

Lin, Y.-H., Chiang, C.-L., Lin, P.-H., Chang, L.-R., Ko, C.-H., Lee, Y.-H., & Lin, S.-H. (2021). Proposed diagnostic criteria for smartphone addiction. PLoS ONE, 16(7), e0254148. https://doi.org/10.1371/journal.pone.0254148

Lindström, B., Tobler, P. N., & Palminteri, S. (2021). Reinforcement learning with social and non-social rewards: A comparative meta-analysis. *Neuroscience & Biobehavioral Reviews, 120*, 141–154. https://doi.org/10.1016/j.neubiorev.2020.11.008

Luna, K. (2019, October). *Speaking of Psychology: How Memory Can Be Manipulated.* Apa.org; American Psychological Association. https://www.apa.org/news/podcasts/speaking-of-psychology/memory-manipulated

Matey, B. (2023, January 19). *The Difference Between Ruminating and Processing Thoughts.* Open Minds Psychological. https://openmindspsychological.com/the-difference-between-ruminating-and-processing-thoughts/

McEwen, B. S. (2007). Physiology and neurobiology of stress and adaptation: central role of the brain. *Physiological Reviews, 87*(3), 873-904. https://doi.org/10.1152/physrev.00041.2006

Meshi, D., Elizarova, A., Bender, A. R., & Verdejo-García, A. (2020). Excessive social media use and its association with decision making deficits. *Journal of Behavioral Addictions, 9*(4), 963–977. https://doi.org/10.1556/2006.2020.00086

Miller, G. E., Chen, E., & Zhou, E. S. (2007). If it goes up, must it come down? Chronic stress and the hypothalamic-pituitary-adrenocortical axis in humans. *Psychoneuroendocrinology, 34*(2), 129-134. https://doi.org/10.1016/j.psyneuen.2008.10.001

Neurolaunch. (2024, March 15). Understanding social media's dopamine addiction. Retrieved from https://neurolaunch.com/social-media-dopamine/

Nolen-Hoeksema et al. (2008): "Rethinking Rumination"

Osorio-Gómez, D., María Isabel Miranda, Kioko Guzmán-Ramos, & Bermúdez-Rattoni, F. (2023). Transforming experiences: Neurobiology of memory updating/editing. *Frontiers in Systems Neuroscience, 17*. https://doi.org/10.3389/fnsys.2023.1103770

Conclusion

Pilat, D., & Krastev, S. (2018). *Illusory truth effect - The Decision Lab*. The Decision Lab. https://thedecisionlab.com/biases/illusory-truth-effect

Puderbaugh, M., & Emmady, P. D. (2023). *Neuroplasticity*. National Library of Medicine; StatPearls Publishing. https://www.ncbi.nlm.nih.gov/books/NBK557811/

Raichle, M. E., et al. (2001). A default mode of brain function. Proceedings of the National Academy of Sciences, 98(2), 676–682. https://doi.org/10.1073/pnas.98.2.676

Rapkoch, K. (2024, December 9). *Trauma Loops: Causes, Symptoms, and Treatment Options*. Www.re-Origin.com. https://www.re-origin.com/conditions/trauma-loops

Reknes, I., Visockaite, G., Liefooghe, A., Lovakov, A., & Einarsen, S. V. (2019). Locus of Control Moderates the Relationship Between Exposure to Bullying Behaviors and Psychological Strain. *Frontiers in Psychology, 10*. https://doi.org/10.3389/fpsyg.2019.01323

Richards, J. M., & Gross, J. J. (2000). Emotion regulation and memory: The cognitive costs of keeping one's cool. *Journal of Personality and Social Psychology, 79*(3), 410–424. https://doi.org/10.1037/0022-3514.79.3.410

Rude, S. S., Wenzlaff, R. M., Gibbs, B., Vane, J., & Whitney, T. (2003). Negative processing biases predict subsequent depressive symptoms. Cognition & Emotion, 16(3), 423–440. https://doi.org/10.1080/02699930143000554

Sayers, W. M., & Sayette, M. A. (2013). Suppression on Your Own Terms. *Psychological Science, 24*(9), 1740–1746. https://doi.org/10.1177/0956797613479977

Schultz, W. (2015). Neuronal reward and decision signals: From theories to data. Physiological Reviews, 95(3), 853–951. https://doi.org/10.1152/physrev.00023.2014

Seligson, S. (2015, August 20). *Elizabeth Loftus on "The Memory Factory."* The Situationist. https://thesituationist.wordpress.com/2015/08/20/elizabeth-loftus-on-the-memory-factory/

Shanava, I., & Gergauli, G. (2022). A Study of Relationship between Locus of Control and Self-monitoring to Resilience in Students. *European Scientific Journal ESJ, 9*. https://doi.org/10.19044/esipreprint.9.2022.p612

Sheline et al. (2009) – "The default mode network and self-referential processes in depression"

Sherman, L. E., Greenfield, P. M., Hernandez, L. M., & Dapretto, M. (2016). Peer influence via Instagram: Effects on brain and behavior in adolescence and young adulthood. Psychological Science, 27(7), 1027–1035. https://doi.org/10.1177/0956797616645673

Stange, J. P., Alloy, L. B., & Fresco, D. M. (2017). Inflexibility as a vulnerability to depression: A systematic qualitative review. Clinical Psychology: Science and Practice, 24(3), 245–276. https://doi.org/10.1111/cpsp.12201

Swinburne University. (2024, January 10). The detrimental neurological effects of doomscrolling: Mounting evidence. Retrieved from https://disa.org/the-detrimental-neurological-effects-of-doomscrolling-mounting-evidence/

Talktoangel. (2024, May 1). *What are the Signs of Toxic Positivity?* TalktoAngel. https://www.talktoangel.com/blog/what-are-the-signs-of-toxic-positivity

Conclusion

Tseng, J., & Poppenk, J. (2020). Brain meta-state transitions demarcate thoughts across task contexts exposing the mental noise of trait neuroticism. Nature communications, 11(1), 3480.

Tversky, A., & Kahneman, D. (1974). Judgment under Uncertainty: Heuristics and Biases. Science.

Twenge, J. M., & Campbell, W. K. (2018). Associations between screen time and lower psychological well-being among children and adolescents: Evidence from a population-based study. Preventive Medicine Reports, 12, 271–283. https://doi.org/10.1016/j.pmedr.2018.10.003

Valkenburg, P. M., Beyens, I., Pouwels, J. L., van Driel, I. I., & Keijsers, L. (2022). Social media use and adolescents' self-esteem: Heading for a person-specific media effects paradigm. Journal of Communication, 72(1), 56–78. https://doi.org/10.1093/joc/jqab039

van der Kolk, B. A. (2014). The body keeps the score: Brain, mind, and body in the healing of trauma. Viking.

WebMD Network. (2024, February 20). Screen fatigue, doom scrolling, and brain fog: Are these new-age Alzheimer's triggers? Doctor explains. Retrieved from https://www.onlymyhealth.com/screen-fatigue-doom-scrolling-and-brain-fog-are-these-newage-alzheimers-triggers-doctor-explains-12977832979

Zofkie, M. (2024, September 23). *Solid Foundations Therapy*. Solid Foundations Therapy. https://www.solidfoundationstherapy.com/blogs/rumination-and-processing-a-guide-to-emotional-clarity

www.ingramcontent.com/pod-product-compliance
Lightning Source LLC
Chambersburg PA
CBHW070643160426
43194CB00009B/1553